THE COMPLETE BOOK OF
AMERICAN COUNTRY ANTIQUES

Katharine M. McClinton

THE COMPLETE BOOK

OF

American Country Antiques

COWARD - McCANN, Inc.
NEW YORK

PRINTED IN THE UNITED STATES OF AMERICA

Contents

⊰ 5 ⊱

Introduction

COUNTRY ANTIQUES has become one of the most popular fields of antique collecting today. Everyone knows about country antiques. They are at the country shows, and summer visitors search dedicatedly for them in Vermont and the other New England states and Pennsylvania. But they are also indigenous to other rural districts throughout the United States.

Country antiques include the household utensils and tools of the plain people—the farmers, artisans, mechanics, tradespeople and keepers of the village stores, all people of humble origins and simple tastes. The articles from their homes and shops and their trade and farm tools were made of native materials. Products crafted by their crude, sturdy tools possess an unsophisticated charm that reflects the skill and ingenuity of the early artisans. There is also a peasant quality about these articles—articles which retain the intrinsic beauty of the materials from which they were made. Moreover, country antiques provide a vivid and detailed picture of early American rural life and the tastes of our ancestors.

Besides the New England farmer and the Western pioneer, there were certain communities of religious sects that lived the simple life and whose articles of everyday living may be classed as country antiques. These include the things made and used by the various Shaker communities, the household articles of the Pennsylvania Dutch, and those made by the Mormons, the Moravians of Salem, North Carolina, and the Zoar communities of Ohio.

For the collector of country antiques a definition that lists their characteristics may be helpful. There are two kinds of country antiques: the early handcrafted pieces and the later factory-made pieces. First, there are the early primitive pieces which were made by native craftsmen, itinerant workers, and country folk. They shaped, whittled, hammered, and spun the necessary articles of simple pioneer living out of natural materials—wood from the forest, clay from the earth, wool from the sheep, flax from the field, and iron, copper, and tin from the mine. All these materials had rough, natural textures and rich earth-toned colors, ranging from coppery red-browns to orange-yellow and red and from clay gray to mineral blue. Early shapes were simple and utilitarian. Simplicity of life made for unadornment. All early country pieces were also made with a specific need in mind, and the crudely shaped article often served the purpose better than a sophisticated product.

Various articles required in the country differed markedly from those used in towns and cities. Thus, certain artisans came into being to serve the needs of the country dweller. First came the housewright and the joiner. In the country the same man—the carpenter—did both jobs. The carpenter made the wooden parts of his tools himself, including his level, square, and mallets. He hewed the oak logs needed to build the house with his ax, dressed the surfaces with an adz, and cut the timber to length with a crosscut saw.

The joining work was done mostly with several kinds of

planes. Joiners also put in window frames, built stairs, made paneling, and frequently put together simple furniture, such as chests and boxes.

The blacksmith was an important country worker. Although most of his work was horseshoeing, he also made the necessary metal parts for the tools of all types of workmen. He made the hoe, the ax, the shovel, and the plowshare. The blacksmith also made a hand-hammered cowbell that collectors search for today. He produced the andirons, fire tongs, poker, and shovel for the fireplace and the fireplace cooking equipment, which included the trivet, gridiron, toaster, pothook, and trammel. Hardware for doors and windows, including bolts, hinges and latches, and the nails to keep them in place were hand-hammered on the anvil.

Barrels, tubs, and pails were used in great quantities, not only on the farm, but also in the house. Although the farmer could hollow out a tree trunk to use for storage, he needed tubs and barrels to store so many different products—flour, cornmeal, cider, maple syrup, salt meat, and fish—that when possible, he bought the tubs and barrels from the village cooper. Barrels were used in the South to ship tobacco, rice, tar, resin, and turpentine. The stains and odors of old barrels often indicate their use.

Other essential country workers included the miller and the tanner. No matter how small the village, there was usually a miller who ground each farmer's grain. The tanner, too, was an indispensable workman in early America because buckskin breeches were worn by all countrymen.

Country families nearly always owned a loom, and the woman of the house wove the flax and wool. But in large families so much cloth was needed that the itinerant weaver was welcomed. He often worked at the simple family loom, making plain, striped, and checked fabrics for clothing, sheets, towels, napkins, tablecloths, and blankets. Wool woven on a linen warp was called linsey-woolsey and was one of the most durable country materials. Plain over-and-under weaving was called tabby. Coverlets were made with cotton warp and woolen welt. The patterns on these overshot coverlets were in contrasting colors, and the names of the designs stir memories of homespun days. Sweetbriar Beauty, Whig Rose, and Blazing Star were some of the simplest.

Another traveling workman was the chandler. Some people made their own candles and could mold as many as a dozen at a time, but the traveling chandler had molds that formed six dozen candles at once. He also made soap out of the softer fat.

Peddlers and itinerant workmen were vital to the farm community. At first they traveled by foot with kits or trunks on their backs, but later they had wagons. The arrival of the peddler's red wagon was always an event. Besides pots, kettles, and baskets, there were toys for the children and needles, thread, and other Yankee notions for the housewife. The most important itinerant worker was the man who mended household articles—the tinker with his charcoal brazier and leather kit of tools, who traveled from house to house, mending leaky pots and pans with solder and rivets, putting new handles on tin dippers, and recasting pewter spoons. His tool kit, with its hammers, tongs, tin snips, hand vise, and soldering iron, is one of the most sought-after collectibles.

Country antiques of different localities take on many regional characteristics. Those of New England reflect the simple homespun life of that region, whereas the antiques found in the West possess a rough-and-ready frontier quality. Also, there is a difference in the items available. Woodenware is found in great quantities in the East; objects of iron and leather are often associated with Western frontier life.

The exact dating of country antiques is difficult because the same shapes and methods of handicraft continued through the years. Moreover, the nineteenth-century artisan often used the tools of his ancestors. The early products were so closely related to use and served their purpose so well that when the machine took over the work of the craftsman, the article was still made in the same form. Butter molds are a good example. At first they were hand-carved, but later the same shapes and designs were factory-made.

These later articles, which include patented nineteenth-century household, farm, and trade products no longer made and thus outdated, constitute the second type of country antiques. The outmoded butter churn, the old hand-washing machine, the apple parer, the sausage stuffer, the nutmeg grater, the flatiron, and the old railroad and coach lanterns— all are collectible country antiques although they may be no more than fifty years old.

There are many aspects to collecting country antiques. You can collect the tools of early trade; the cranes, trivets, and cooking pots that made up the hardware of the hearth; or the kitchen stove and its utensils of iron, tin, and copper. The articles used in harvesting the crops, the buckets and molds of the Vermont maple sugar industry, the utensils used in making butter, or the laundry tubs, washboards, scrubbing sticks, and clothespins for washing and drying clothes would form an interesting and instructive collection. You can collect antiques for use in the decorating and furnishing of your house. You can also collect purely for the decorative beauty of an object's material, shape, or color. This sort of collecting calls for considerable discrimination and usually results in the most interesting and valuable collections.

I

Tinware

Still Life with Lanterns, *by John Frederick Peto.*
BROOKLYN MUSEUM.

TINWARE PLAYED an important role in early America. Tin camp plates, canteens, and kettles were used by the Revolutionary Army. Some were imported from England, but many were made in America. In 1777 and 1778 several New York tin-plate workers advertised "camp dishes and plates," and many other advertisements in early newspapers give evidence of the tinsmith and of the numerous articles he made. A long list taken from the advertisement of Thomas Passmore, of Philadelphia, in the *Federal Gazette,* November 30, 1793, is quoted by Henry J. Kauffman in the *Concise Encyclopedia of American Antiques.* The articles included ale tasters and ovens, candle molds, candlesticks, dustpans, egg slicers, funnels, graters, gingerbread cutters, hearing trumpets, lamps and lanterns, "moulds for blomonges," milk strainers, pails, and saucepans, ovens, pepperboxes, sugar boxes, soup ladles, stills, tureens, and waterpots.

Edward Pattison is credited with establishing the first manufactory of tinware in Berlin, Connecticut, in 1770. This tinware was mostly for household uses, and Pattison peddled his wares from door to door in baskets, on horseback, and later in wagons drawn by horses. The story of the tin peddler

Coffee roaster for top of stove. INDEX
OF AMERICAN DESIGN.

Sausage stuffer, tin and wood.
OLD STURBRIDGE VILLAGE.

Tin reflector oven.
OLD STURBRIDGE VILLAGE.

with his red cart, tin horn, and stock of tin utensils and other sundry wares has often been told, and a wealth of lore surrounds the tin peddler of eighteenth- and nineteenth-century America.

Although the tin peddler's stock included a wide variety of items, tinware for the collector today may be grouped under three main headings: tinware for the hearth, tinware for the stove and pantry, and tinware for lighting. Each category includes a long list of articles for today's collector, and the most valuable collection would be one that focuses on a single field.

Some of the most interesting tinware articles were those used on the hearth, which also included some of the earliest handmade items. Although the staple cooking utensils for the hearth were iron, tinware ovens provided a new means of cooking, and as early as 1781 "newly constructed Salisbury kitchens for baking, boiling, and roasting" were on the American market. However, the simpler roasting oven with revolving spit was used more often. Sometimes the spit was placed between the andirons or hung over the fire, and then a tin drip pan was placed underneath to catch the juices. There were also small reflecting roasters for birds and apple roasters. Biscuit and cracker bakers were small square ovens set on legs with a pan or shelf to hold the biscuits and a hinged cover. All these tin ovens are rare. There were also tin gridirons, corn poppers, coffee-bean roasters, and covered pans to carry embers. Plate warmers with several shelves for plates, a door, iron ring handles, and shapely Queen Anne legs are museum pieces. And small plate warmers called tin bonnets covered plates of food set on the hearth. All the early tinware was made by hand, but later roasters, such as coffee-bean roasters, are sometimes found marked with the name of a manufacturer.

Tin foot stoves made of pierced sheets of tin stood on the hearth ready to be filled with embers. They were round or square with handles. Later ones had wooden frames with supports of turned wood at the corners. Larger foot warmers were made for the use of two persons, and small tin warmers, as well as tightly covered warmers that held hot water, were designed to be carried in a muff. Tin warming pans similar to the early copper and brass warming pans were made in the late nineteenth century.

When cookstoves came into common use in the nineteenth century, new types of kitchen utensils were designed for use on the top of the stove. Tin teakettles were intended to sit on the flat top of the stove or to fit over the open stove hole. Such articles as coffee-bean roasters were to be set into the stove hole nearer the coals. The early-nineteenth-century cook welcomed the advent of tinware, and the heavy iron pots and pans were quickly replaced by tin cooking utensils. Tin-covered pots, tin coffeepots, pitchers, pie pans, muffin pans, cake and pudding molds, covered cans for baking both brown and white bread, and pitchers and cups of various sizes—all were made by hand by the early tinsmiths. Later similar articles were machine-made.

The tin coffeepot is one of the pieces collectors covet most because it includes pots of various sizes and shapes, both decorated and plain. Pennsylvania Dutch coffeepots ornamented with punched designs of hearts, birds, tulips, and hex signs often had the maker's name punched on the pot. These designs were usually made with hammer and nails but were not cut through the tin. Any pot with the initials, name, or

Tin teakettle. Nineteenth century.
HENRY FORD MUSEUM.

*Tinware coffeepot with punched
decoration. Nineteenth century.*
METROPOLITAN MUSEUM OF ART.

*Group of tinware: hogback candlesticks, whale-oil can with angled spout,
cups and coffeepots made by Shakers.* INDEX OF AMERICAN DESIGN.

date of the owner or maker is rare, and those with such makers' names as J. Ketterer, W. Schade, or M. Uebele, made in the 1830's and 1840's, are probably in museums. Painted tin teapots were also produced in both New England and Pennsylvania; but these pieces were usually for display, not for everyday use, and they will be discussed along with other decorative tinware.

Utilitarian undecorated tinware also included dippers, scoops, strainers, sifters, chopping knives, cottage cheese molds, and graters. The Pennsylvania Dutch cottage cheese molds with pierced and slit designs are especially popular with collectors today. Made in square, diamond, round, and heart shapes, these molds continue to be popular, and new ones may still be bought in Pennsylvania. The old molds were made of heavy tin with a dull surface, and their perforated designs were made with old square-cut nails. Early graters were also pierced with decorative designs, usually geometric dots, dashes and circles. Later graters had all-over piercing. Such foods as potatoes or carrots required large graters, but the most interesting are the little nutmeg graters. Some of these, set on wooden bases, were made in the mid-eighteenth century. Nutmeg graters are of various sizes, including miniature ones that could be carried in the vest pocket and used to flavor drinks. Many graters, made to hang from a loop handle of tin or by a hole cut in the crested top, were patented and manufactured in the late nineteenth century and are a type still used. Pie crimpers, for cutting around the edge of the pie, were a combination of tin and wood. Some had wooden wheels with tin handles; others had tin wheels or tin wheels combined with handles of wood. The serrations of the wheels made attractive designs. Closely asso-

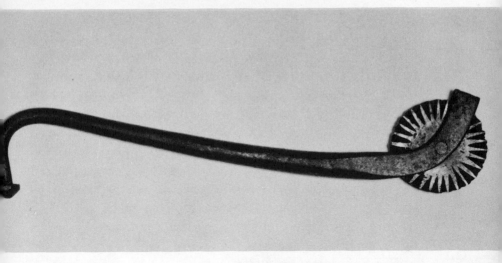

Pie crimpers with tin wheels. HENRY FRANCIS DU PONT
WINTERTHUR MUSEUM.

ciated with the baking of pies was cookie making, and for this there were innumerable cookie cutters. Early ones had fluted edges, and the various shapes included stars, crescents, hearts, diamonds, flowers, leaves, animals, and human figures. The Revolutionary soldier, the Indian, William Penn, and the horseback rider—all were favorites. Later figures included Uncle Sam, the forty-niner, fat men, baseball players, and top hats. Cookie cutters continue to be made, but you can tell the old handmade cutter from the factory-made model by its workmanship. The early cook had many other articles of tinware. There were tin beaters and whippers of various kinds, tin sausage guns, meat pressers, and wine pressers.

The home laundry had several utensils of tin, including a gadget with a tin suction cup, a tin washboard, and a tin holder for irons to be heated on top of the stove. For the bedroom there were tin washbasins and pitchers, tin soap dishes, tin shaving mugs, and a tin chamber pot with its own tin box, as well as a tin bedpan for the sick. A collection of tin dairy equipment could include milk pans, milk cans, butter churns, cream whippers, and ice-cream freezers. Tin boxes were of various sizes, ranging from small containers for spices and other commodities to covered tin lunch pails. Tin trunks and hatboxes were made for traveling.

Tin was an important material for making lighting devices of all kinds. There were early vertical and round tin sconces that hung flat against the wall and held candles. Tin chandeliers swung from the ceiling and held a group of candles in their branching sockets. These handmade chandeliers are rare. There were also tin candlesticks, lamps, and lanterns. Candlesticks were of various types; the chamber candlestick had a saucer with a tin loop handle and a gadget for adjust-

Tin chandelier. METROPOLITAN MUSEUM OF ART.

ing the flame. The ones with large saucers are the rarest. There were also candlesticks with flat round bases and some with inverted bases, called hog scrapers. An interesting early candleholder was set in the lid of a tinderbox, which held the tinder used to light the candle before matches were invented. Tin candle molds were made in many styles and sizes. Some produced a single candle, and others as many as a dozen. Round molds are rare, and so are molds with cutwork borders on their top rims. Tin skimmers for skimming the tallow and cups with handles for scooping and pouring it into the molds are also available. Oblong cylinder candleboxes with sliding covers held a reserve supply, and a snuffer and tray were needed to keep the candle in condition. Snuffers were made of steel, but the trays were of tin, often decorated with a lacquered design. Unusual candle holders included the miner's candle which had a hook for fastening to the miner's cap, the rare Bible lamp candleholder, and the candlestand with a base standard and a tin shade which was the ancestor of the student lamp.

A collector of tin lamps will start with the early simple Betty lamp, which resembles an antique pottery cresset lamp but hangs on a chain. There are also rare Betty lamps on stands. A great variety of tin lamps—round, cylinder, and acorn types—were developed after the Betty lamp. In the mid-nineteenth century there were swinging lamps for torchlight processions, early railroad lamps, and table lamps with tin shades. Tin lanterns also came in a variety of sizes and shapes. The Paul Revere lantern is oblong with a pierced "steeple." The ordinary decorative pierced lantern with a cone top is seen in many shops. Tin lanterns with glass windows and those with a glass globe and tin base, top, and loop handle are also available; they are often found with the maker's name stamped in the tin base. Nurse's lamps with handles and a kettle and cup were used in the Civil War. There was also a tin traveling lamp similar to today's canned-heat burner. Tin matchboxes that hang on the wall are plentiful. Early ones were handmade; later they were machine-made in the factory.

Although we have been listing the old and for the most part rare pieces of tinware, the collector should not neglect the later factory-made pieces, which are more important for their historical significance than for their workmanship. Even such small articles as beaters reveal an ever-changing form, and late patented pieces dated and with such advertising as a grocer's name, or a spoon or pie pan bearing the name of a bakery are collector's pieces.

The ordinary tin lantern that was used on the farm and hung outside the kitchen door ready for early milking or late chores at the barn is now a collector's item. Late nutmeg graters, tin cups, children's ABC tin plates, doughnut cutters with wooden handles, dustpans, egg beaters, the match safe marked with the maker's name or patent date—all late articles but no longer made—will fit into a collection of interesting, if not rare, tinware.

In the mid-nineteenth century—that era of souvenirs and remembrance gifts—articles of tin were made for the tin wedding anniversary. The trade card of Musgrove and Son, New York City, read: "Tin Goods for Wedding Presents—Emblematical of Different Trades and Professions." As may be imagined, the articles included not only those related to the trade or profession, but also humorous gifts intended to recall episodes in the life of the couple. The complete collection of tin articles given to Mr. and Mrs. F. F. Thompson on their

Tin lantern. Pennsylvania, about 1770. METROPOLITAN MUSEUM OF ART.

Tin lantern with green bull's-eye glass. Pennsylvania, about 1825. METROPOLITAN MUSEUM OF ART.

Tin wall sconce with tooled decoration. Eighteenth century. METROPOLITAN MUSEUM OF ART.

Tin candle boxes. METROPOLITAN MUSEUM OF ART.

tin wedding anniversary in 1867 is in the Ontario County Historical Society, Canandaigua, New York. Here is the list of articles in the collection:

Crown	Watch and chain
Spring bonnet	Playing cards
Two stovepipe hats	Picture frames
Egg cooker and timer	Lady's slippers
Strongbox	Necktie
Fruit dish	Funnels
Pipe	Book cover
Hand mirror	Teaspoons
Rosary and crucifix	Goblet
Pudding mold	Stein
Cookie cutters	Fan
Tray	Bric-a-brac shelves
Birdbath	Toys and miniatures

Painted Tinware: The early tinware business centered in Connecticut and Maine, which produced most painted tinware, but some tinware was decorated in neighboring New York and Vermont and in Pennsylvania Dutch country. Tinware could be decorated by two methods—japanning and stenciling. Japanning originated in China and was introduced in the eighteenth century into England and thence into America. Tin articles were coated with asphaltum varnish, which produced a shiny, transparent, brownish-black effect. Then the article was heat-dried and the hand-painted decoration applied. Stencil decoration was done by applying paint or bronze with a pouncer through a cardboard cutout design. The work was done in colored bronzes and oil paints, using such colors as yellow ocher, Indian red, Prussian blue, and black and white. Designs included flowers, fruits, birds, trees, animals, houses, boats, and people.

Although tinware was used as a utilitarian ware in the homes of the well-to-do, it served as a substitute for silver and plate in the homes of the less affluent and in rural districts. Painted tinware was especially treasured in the country for its decorative qualities and was handed down as a family heirloom so that much has survived in fairly good condition. The best-known decorator of early tinware was Zachariah Stevens, who operated a shop in Maine from 1798 to 1842. The designs painted on tinware at Stevens Plains were realistic and soft in color. Two large dull vermilion cherries appeared on many of the pieces, and some had yellow and cream backgrounds. The designs were applied both with stencils and freehand. The pieces included cakeboxes, trays of all kinds, tea caddies, tea and coffeepots, pincushions, and trinket boxes.

In Berlin, Connecticut, Hiram Mygatt and Oliver Buckley painted the tinware made by Edward and William Pattison. Buckley's pieces are identified by a center spot of chrome orange surrounded by small dots and heart-shaped leaves. The pieces also had running borders of red, green, and black on white bands. But the most easily recognized Berlin pieces are stenciled coffin-shaped trays, small flattop boxes, tea caddies, bread trays, flower holders, cakeboxes, and apple trays, which often had red, blue, and green backgrounds with vermilion stripes. The bread trays were oblong and had straight sides and rolled ends. Elliptical trays with pointed ends were for crackers. The apple trays are square with curving fan-shaped sides. Some trays had latticework sides. The trinket boxes were richly decorated and had a hasp for a padlock. Canisters for tea and coffee were of various sizes and shapes—round, square, and oblong. Some were hand-deco-

Painted tin coffeepot. INDEX OF AMERICAN DESIGN.

Painted tin nurse's lamp. Pennsylvania. INDEX OF AMERICAN DESIGN.

Painted tin tray. Pennsylvania. INDEX OF AMERICAN DESIGN.

rated, and others were marked "Tea" or "Coffee" with a hand stencil. Later they were factory-made.

The Butler family of East Greenville, New York, were also painters of tinware. Ann Butler specialized in clocks and clock faces, as well as tinware, and often initialed her pieces.

Much tinware was painted in Pennsylvania. It differed in both color and design from New England tinware. New England tinware was distinguished by light blues, pinks, greens, and lavenders and by its delicate brushwork, whereas that of Pennsylvania displayed bold colors; bright red, yellow, and emerald green, and it had characteristic simple designs. Motifs included red and yellow tulips, peaches, tomatoes, gold and green leaves, distelfinks, and hex signs, whereas designs of delicate flowers, urns, and weeping willows and designs inspired by the Orient were found on New England tinware. The tin articles painted in Pennsylvania included tea caddies, tea and coffeepots, mugs, covered boxes, trays of all sizes and shapes, candlesticks, nutmeg graters, salt shakers, and cream pitchers.

Perhaps the most popular piece of decorated tinware was the tray. Tin trays were made in all sizes and shapes from the simple coffin-shaped country tray with a middle seam to the Chippendale scallop-edged tray with elaborate Oriental designs of birds and flowers. The Queen Anne tray had rounded points on the scalloped edge. There were also early lace-edged trays with pierced sides. Oval and oblong galley trays had simple border designs and solid edges with handholes. There were also small snuffer trays to hold tin or steel snuffers.

The tin spice box is another favorite with collectors. They came in sets held in a round covered box, and they were usually stenciled with bronze paint. Larger spice boxes with elaborate decorations were used in country stores. Painted tinware reached the height of its popularity about the middle of the nineteenth century, and numerous small factories produced painted tinware. They included the American Tea Tray Works, Albany, New York, and Hull and Stafford, Clinton, Connecticut, which manufactured painted children's toys. Toys were a particularly popular tin item. Made in great numbers in America between 1840 and 1900, they included dolls' furniture, stoves with tiny pots and pans, animals, soldiers, carts, boats, trains, horse-drawn vehicles, and banks. Toys were painted in gay colors, partly by hand and partly by stencil. Although produced cheaply in great quantities, they are scarce and expensive today. Those with bells or mechanisms are particularly sought-after by toy collectors. Many were made as late as the 1920's.

The collector should be warned that there are reproductions of tinware on the market and that decorating tinware has become a popular hobby. The new tinware is heavier than earlier tinware, and the work—too perfect to be handmade—is done by machine. This is particularly noticeable in the edges of trays and in pierced work and lace-edge trays and baskets. New tinware edges are welded together, whereas those of the old pieces lap over. Little tinware is found in perfect condition today, but one should concentrate on securing pieces in good condition rather than on trying to sort pieces from definite localities. Teapots, coffeepots, and trays in good condition are expensive, but small articles, such as covered boxes and mugs, are less costly and more available. Black and brown backgrounds are the most common, and the lighter cream backgrounds are the rarest, most expensive, and least available.

II

Woodenware

Group of woodenware and baskets made by Shakers. CELESTE AND
EDWARD KOSTER.

THE EARLY SETTLERS brought their woodenware dishes, spoons, and trenchers from England. Because the first colonists included turners and coopers, some woodenware was made in America from the earliest times. There is a distinction between the wooden articles made by turners and those made by coopers. Turners' wares included plates, bowls, and other articles turned on the lathe; these articles are now known as treen. Coopers made kegs, tubs, barrels, buckets, and churns. There were various kinds of coopers; tight coopers made barrels for liquids, usually out of oak, and slack coopers made buckets, tubs, and boxes to hold dry materials. They used such woods as ash, maple, elm, chestnut, and hickory. Cedar coopers made churns, buckets, and small articles of cedar. Early-eighteenth-century New York inventories included cedar tubs, churns, bowls, mortars, pails, rundlets, wooden trays, wooden bottles, "knot" and "root bowls," and trenchers. One inventory listed "cuppors tools."

Early America had plenty of wood, including ash, birch, beech, hickory, oak, pine, walnut, poplar, maple, basswood, cedar, maple, and such fruitwoods as apple and cherry, and the settlers soon learned which to use for each article. Ash was strong and served to make hoops on barrels and kegs. Birch was used for boxes, clothes pins, pegs, and pail handles. Beech was reddish and was made into scoops, rolling pins, and boxes. Hickory was split and used for baskets. Pine was good for furniture, boxes, and small kitchen utensils. Oak was heavy and well suited for casks, large boxes, and butter churns. Poplar was made into bowls, plates, spoons, and scoops. Maple, the most popular of all woods, was used for butter molds, mashers, stirrers, scoops, and bowls.

There were coopers and turners in all large cities by the nineteenth century. In 1824 Edward Arents advertised a cedar ware manufactory in the New York *Commercial Advertiser*. He made "Pails, Churns, Tubs, Coolers and Bathing Tubs, brass, iron, and wood bound." Gideon Cox operated a large woodenware manufactory in Philadelphia from 1825 to 1840. He made bathtubs, bowls, churns, butter prints, curly bowls, buckets, and cedarware. However, even at this early date the woodenware industry was centered in New Hampshire, Vermont, and Massachusetts. Rindge, New Hampshire, specialized in wooden bandboxes, spice boxes, and white birch clothespins. Mortars, pestles, and chopping bowls were made at Jaffrey, and dishes, spoons, breadboards, mugs, and trays at Weare, New Hampshire. In Massachusetts, Winchendon became the woodenware center of the world in the mid-nineteenth century, and Hingham became known for the Hingham bucket. There were differences between the woodenware made in various parts of the country. Local cooking practices differed, and implements and utensils varied accordingly. Articles made by the New York Dutch and the Pennsylvania Germans, influenced by their European peasant backgrounds, had carving and painted decorations, whereas the New Eng-

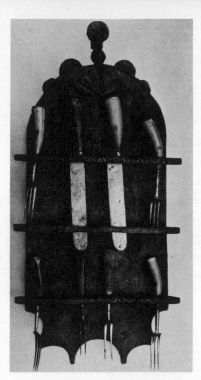

Carved rack with elk-handled knives and forks. Pennsylvania, early nineteenth century. METRO-POLITAN MUSEUM OF ART.

Carved poplar spoon rack. Pennsylvania, early nineteenth century. METROPOLITAN MUSEUM OF ART.

Wooden pipe boxes. Early nineteenth century. WADSWORTH ATHENEUM.

landers, especially the Shakers, guided by religious scruples, produced strictly plain articles without carving or other adornment. The Pennsylvania Dutch delighted in wood carving, and many articles of household use, such as spoons, ladles, salt and spice boxes, butter molds, pie markers, and spoon racks, were carved with designs, including the tulip, heart, or hex wheel, as well as with initials and dates.

The carved spoon racks, made to hang on the wall, were especially decorative. These rectangular vertical racks, decorated with scratch carving of hex circles, spiral wheels, stars, and herringbone designs, had narrow notched shelves, into which spoons were hung. The top was usually crested with a cutout design of wheels, and there was often a drawer below to hold knives. These racks were different from the regular knife box in that the bars to hold knives were slotted, not pierced. These racks were often marked with dates and initials and painted blue with the pattern picked out in red, green, white, and yellow. They were made in the Hudson and Delaware valleys, as well as in Pennsylvania. There were other wall boxes, including the knife box, the salt box, the pipe box, and the box that held the comb and brush. Unlike the spoon rack, these boxes were usually plain, except for the cutout at the top, which served as a handle. They were made of pine or walnut.

Shaker pipe boxes and other wall pieces were usually made of pine. Although they had no carving, their excellently proportioned shapes and fine workmanship make them desirable. Henry DeWitte, a mechanic and joiner at New Lebanon, wrote the following in his journal for February 13, 1828: "made a box duff taled it read for the cover and bottom. . . . Feb. 14. I finished the said box. It was for Moses M. to put pipe stems in." The Shaker pipe rack was severely plain; its oval top had a small round hole so that the rack could be hung on the wall. The pipe box was an enclosed rectangle with a small drawer at the bottom. Both rack and box were made of pine. The candle and sewing boxes were also of pine, and there were berry boxes and kitchen boxes as well. Other Shaker woodenware for household use included bowls, spoons, trenchers, mortars and pestles, rolling pins, measuring sticks, spools, table boards for hot dishes, foot warmers, sconces, clothespins, broom, mop and knife handles, and canes.

The garden seed and medicinal herb industries, required thousands of shallow boxes made of thin strips of wood. These boxes were of maple with pine tops and bottoms. Shaker boxes may be identified by the pointed finger laps and the copper nails used for fastening. Boxes were made in nests of twelve, nine, seven, and five. Sometimes there are traces of red, blue, green, yellow or gray vegetable paint on the old boxes. Those made by the early colonists were fastened with hand-cut nails, but they had straight seam laps. The staves were fastened either with buttonhole laps, with one end fitting into a hole at the other end of the lap, or with an arrowpoint overlapping lock. Other woods employed by the Shakers for small household articles included curly or bird's-eye maple for chopping bowls, oval boxes, small tools, and mirror frames, ash for sieve rims; and walnut for basket rims. "Lingumvite" and "willow for spools" were mentioned in the journal of the Shaker craftsman DeWitte.

Woodenware may be divided into different categories according to its use. There is the woodenware used in the house and the woodenware of the trades, of industry, and of farming. The serious collector will want to specialize be-

Poplar wood dough trough. Pennsylvania, early nineteenth century.
INDEX OF AMERICAN DESIGN.

Wooden apple parer. OLD STURBRIDGE VILLAGE.

Butter paddle made by Shakers. INDEX OF AMERICAN DESIGN.

Wooden butter churn. HENRY
FORD MUSEUM.

Covered bucket. INDEX OF
AMERICAN DESIGN.

Early wooden churn.
HENRY FORD MUSEUM.

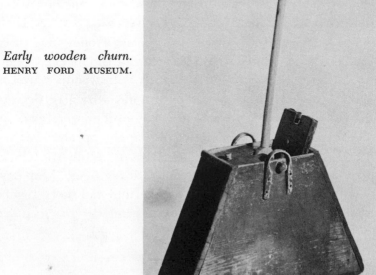

cause the field is large. The woodenware used in the house is further divided into several categories according to its use. There are the woodenware utensils needed for preparing and cooking food. Another group includes containers for storing food, and still another consists of the utensils for eating. Woodenware articles for making bread included the bread trough for kneading the bread, the paddle for stirring the dough, and the long wooden knife for cutting the dough into loaves. Wooden peels, or shovels, were used to put the bread into the oven and to remove it when baked.

Milking and buttermaking required many wooden articles, including the pail for milking; the keelers, or shallow tubs, into which milk was set for the cream to rise; the cream skimmer; and the sour cream tub for storing the cream until ready for buttermaking. Then there was the butter churn, the scoop for taking the butter out of the churn, the butter-worker tray and paddles, and finally the butter molds and prints. Butter churns were made of both pottery and wood. Wooden churns were round, barrel-shaped, or rectangular; the first churn had a paddle that moved up and down, but later inventions included rocking and swinging paddles. Early churns had a natural wood finish, but later ones were often painted red, decorated, and printed with the maker's name. The butter print is extremely popular with woodenware collectors because of the workmanship and attractive designs. The early prints were hand-cut; later on, they were made in factories. The designs included pineapples, pears, cherries, wheat, acorns, tulips, leaves, stars, hearts, geometric circles and triangles, and rare swans, eagles, doves, hens, sheep, and cows. Butter prints were usually round and had short, turned handles. Pennsylvania Dutch butter print designs included

Butter molds. Early nineteenth century.
NEW YORK HISTORICAL SOCIETY.

Wooden ladle. NEW YORK HISTORICAL
SOCIETY.

Wooden scoop. NEW YORK HISTORICAL
SOCIETY.

tulips, hearts, hex signs, three feathers, and a rare cow standing under a huge strawberry blossom. There was also a whole set of articles used for cheese making; these included cheese drainers, sieves, curd knives, cheese ladders, baskets, and the cheese press.

Woodenware was equally important to the housewife in baking cakes, pies, and cookies. There were several types of rolling pins, made of various woods, including the favorite maple, cherry, beech, and pine, as well as mahogany and lignum vitae. There were also grooved cookie rollers. Some rolling pins had intaglio designs, which were transferred to the dough. And carved springerle molds were popular for decorating cakes. The patterns included flowers, birds, and animals. For making pies there were pie crimpers, consisting of a small fluted wheel fastened to a handle. Those made by the Pennsylvania Dutch were carved with incised line designs and sometimes included dates and initials.

Various sizes of scoops, spoons, pounders, and mashers were also necessary for food preparation. Mashers included huge ones for making sauerkraut, smaller ones for potatoes and other vegetables, and very small toddy sticks; mashers were made of maple, both curly and bird's-eye, walnut, and lignum vitae. The heads of meat pounders were marked off in square lines. Most interesting of all the food-preparing implements were the mortar and pestle, made of burl maple and lignum vitae, and used for pounding herbs, sugar, spice, and salt. The mortar and pestle were turned on the lathe and decorated with encircling lines. There were also large grain and corn mortars. Wooden scoops included those for cream, grease, and apple butter, and a rectangular scoop was made for scooping soap. A great variety of scoops were used for flour, meal, and sugar. Wooden skimmers, dippers, funnels, and a long-handled hasty-pudding spoon were also available.

Apples were an important commodity of the early American home. They were plentiful and versatile; dried, they were made into apple butter and applesauce, as well as apple pies. Apples also furnished vinegar for cooking and cider for drinking. Almost all the implements for making the various apple products and storage containers were made of wood. Apples were dried in baskets and frames of narrow slats, or they were hung on sticks between hooks on the rafters. When products such as apple butter were made, the apples had to be pared. Early apple parers were made of wood, but later they had metal wheels set in a wooden base. Although most apple parers were made for use on the table, some were mounted on a bench. Later patented machines not only peeled the apples, but cored them as well. Applesauce and apple butter were made and sold in great quantities by the Shakers. Shaker apple butter scoops, spoons, and stirrers were simple and beautiful in design, and they are much sought-after by collectors. The apple butter was stored in buckets. Cider was made on a wooden press and trickled into buckets. It was then stored in wooden barrels.

Meat preparation was also a necessary household job. For this there was a wooden meat grinder and wooden and tin sausage guns. Another task that required wooden implements was the making of soft soap and the washing of clothes. For clothes washing there were scrubbing sticks and wooden washboards. The wooden pounders and washtubs that preceded the first washing machines were handmade. For ironing clothes the wooden smoothing board preceded the flatiron,

Turned wooden trenchers. METROPOL-
ITAN MUSEUM OF ART.

Wooden pitcher. NEW YORK HIS-
TORICAL SOCIETY.

Turned wooden bowl with cover.
NEW YORK HISTORICAL SOCIETY.

Wooden mortars. METROPOLI-
TAN MUSEUM OF ART.

*Wooden spice grinder. Early
nineteenth century.* NEW YORK
HISTORICAL SOCIETY.

and wooden clothes line frames, winders, and clothespins were both handmade and lathe-turned.

Woodenware of every kind is popular with collectors today, but because of its interesting shapes, the beauty of its natural woods, and its patina and hand turning, treenware is the favorite, as well as most attractive, form of woodenware. Treenware consists of those pieces of woodenware used in serving and eating food—bowls of many dimensions, trenchers or plates, platters, cups, noggins, tankards, pitchers, spoons and scoops of many sizes, individual salt dishes, and covered sugar bowls. The bowls were usually hand-turned on the lathe. Burl maple and ash bowls were usually early; later factory-made bowls were generally of chestnut, although some were of maple or pine. Large long chopping bowls were seldom made of burl and were usually not hand-hewn. Some bowls had covers with ornamental finials. Trenchers or plates were usually round or oval. Spoons were made both with straight and with graceful curved handles; a few had carved handles.

Coopers were also furnished many articles for household use. Coopers ware is not as interesting as other woodenware. It is less artistic, often crude and unattractive. The pieces consisted of small staves held together by two or three hoops with a peg slipped through a hole to hold the handle. There were sugar buckets made of pine with ash or hickory hoops, water buckets including well buckets, and buckets to carry water. The piggin was a small bucket with a stave handle used as a dipper for water or to carry food to small farm animals. Butter churns were also made by coopers, and they were staved and hooped. Coopers turned out small kegs for water, rundlets for rum, canteens, and oyster kegs; the water and rum kegs had wire or leather handles. They also produced various sizes of tubs and keelers; the keelers had short stave handles with handle holes. Besides the larger buckets, kegs, and tubs, coopers made tankards and pitchers for use at the table. These usually had a hand-carved handle. As a rule, all these tubs, barrels, keelers, and tankards were made by professional coopers, but there were also substitutes hollowed and whittled out of logs by the man of the house.

Many wooden implements and smaller articles were used in home industry about the farm and in the trades. Some are too large to be discussed in a book about small antiques, but the group of objects used in spinning and weaving is so closely related to the household and includes so many small pieces of woodenware of the homespun and country type that they are included. There were small spinning wheels for flax and combs, or hackles, which were hand-hewn boards with nails for sorting the flax according to fineness. Wool was carded on a similar board. Spinning wheels for wool were larger than flax wheels, and there were small hand spindles as well.

There were also several types of reels of four or six spokes set on a stand, spools for yarn, and racks to hold the spools. There were small looms, for weaving braid, tape, and cloth; bobbin winders; and shuttles, sometimes made of dogwood. Small Pennsylvania Dutch tape looms often had decorative carving, as well as names and dates.

Vermont's early maple sugar industry used wooden buckets, tin buckets were used later on. The wooden sap bucket is identified by one protruding stave with a hole, by which it could be hung to the tree. Buckets for carrying the sap had two protruding staves with holes and a stick handle. The shoul-

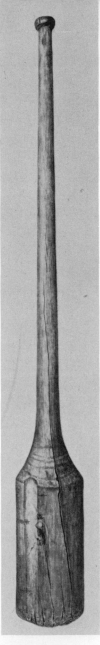

Mallet used to drive bung in wooden cask.
INDEX OF AMERICAN DESIGN.

Sauerkraut
masher. INDEX
OF AMERICAN
DESIGN.

Burl maple bowl. Early nineteenth century.
HENRY FORD MUSEUM.

der yoke used to carry them has become a popular item with collectors. It is hung on the wall or used on the table filled with flowers or fruits. Large molds for maple sugar were divided into small square compartments.

Wooden articles used in cattle and sheep raising included hobbles, yokes, collars, stakings, and stencils for marking sheep. Such industries as fishing and whaling also employed many articles made of wood. And the wooden forms required by cobblers for making shoes are unusual items, as are the forms for gloves and hats.

Articles of woodenware that possess a fine grain and patina are especially attractive. Well proportioned forms, together with fine workmanship, give some articles a primitive art value. Others are valued because few are to be found. Although early woodenware with patina and fine workmanship is particularly desirable, late items, such as potato mashers which are no longer made, are collectible. Any wooden article of Shaker or Pennsylvania Dutch origin has an additional value. Old pieces of woodenware show the marks of the tools, whereas later factory-made articles are smoother. Wooden pegs and hand-forged nails also reveal an article as handmade. Often, the sides of old bowls and dippers are uneven, showing scratches and stains of use. Knot or burl bowls or mortars are rare, and pieces made of curly or bird's-eye maple are few. Any pieces with a date, initials, or carving are scarce and desirable.

Baskets and Produce Boxes: Baskets have been used in America since the earliest times. They were essential in the many tasks about the farm and in the house and saw service later for packaging and getting produce to market. The colonists undoubtedly learned basket weaving from the Indians, although baskets were in common use on the European continent for centuries before America was discovered. The Bible mentions them; the grape-gathering baskets of Jeremiah and the baskets of loaves and fishes in the New Testament are familiar to most people. Baskets are also portrayed in works of art, from the catacomb frescoes of the third century and the mosaic pavements of the fifth century to the present. Baskets in early painting, mosaics, and sculpture are usually of braided design.

American baskets were of several types: those made of splint, from the stripped bark of trees, and reed and rush baskets, of which the willow basket was the most common variety. The Indians made splint baskets of ash and white oak. All the early Colonial splint baskets were also made of ash or white oak. There were many kinds of splint basket. Cheese baskets were round; they featured open hexagon weaving and had bound hoops to strengthen their tops. Utility baskets, such as egg baskets, had a handle that reached across the top of the basket. Other baskets had handgrip handles, one on each side of the top rim. Baskets for gathering clams were square and had hickory handles nailed to the rim with tin supports, the old ones had hand-cut nails. Apple-drying baskets were of two types—round baskets, called cobweb baskets, for drying apples in the house and long flat splint baskets for drying them on the windowsill. The fish basket is similar to the apple-drying basket but deeper, with a sturdy hickory handle. Baskets used for winnowing grain were made in the shape of a scoop with a hickory frame and handles and a splint filling. There were also winnowing sieves, with woven bottoms and splint wooden sides, and square sieves for charcoal. Vinegar funnels and eeltraps were also woven of splint.

Many other kinds of utility baskets—some round, some square, some oblong—were made of splint. A lanternlike basket held flax; a loom basket held bobbins for weaving; other baskets held shuttles; and there were sewing baskets with handles and lids. Even the children had baskets to carry, and miniature baskets were made for their dolls. French willow baskets were imported during the early nineteenth century. Fancy covered oval baskets with a handle and tall ones with a stepped pagodalike cover were of French make. In 1841 Étienne Philipoteaux was making fancy baskets in New York, and by 1846 there were two more fancy basketmakers in New York. Not only were fancy baskets unusual in shape; they also had woven or painted designs, and they were often threaded with satin ribbon. Thirteen basketmakers were listed in the New York directory in 1844. In 1880 there were fifty basketmakers, five dealers, and ten importers, and Charles Zinn & Co. was listed as a basket manufacturer. Three basketmakers were located in Weare, New Hampshire, in 1823, and this part of the country later became a basketmaking center, whose products were distributed throughout the East.

Peddlers used baskets to sell fruits and other produce in New York and such other cities as Philadelphia and Boston from the early nineteenth century on. These baskets were illustrated in the various books of early cries of New York. Bread was sold in large baskets, three or four to a handcart. Hot muffins, tea rusk, hot corn, and fish were also peddled in baskets of varying sizes, the largest being the fish basket. Little girls carried radishes in baskets on their arms or heads, calling from door to door. Strawberries, according to the *Cries of New York, 1816,* were gathered in small baskets hold-

Group of Shaker baskets. INDEX OF AMERICAN DESIGN.

ing from half a pint to a pint. Strawberry baskets were covered with leaves, and a dozen or more were strung on long poles and peddled by women who cried, "Fine ripe strawberries." Later the small baskets were packed in a larger one with a handle and carried on the arm. The basket peddler loaded his wares in a wagon, and according to *Cries of New York, 1834,* his cry was:

> Baskets, wooden bowls
> Of well-chosen wood
> For a kitchen utensil
> You'll find very good.

At this time Gideon Cox was the best-known basket manufacturer and dealer in Philadelphia, and Charles Zinn & Co. was New York's largest manufacturer. Alexander Anderson, who illustrated one of the editions of *Cries of New York* and also did woodcuts for numerous other books and advertisements of the nineteenth century, showed various kinds of baskets in his illustrations and recorded the different uses and the popular craze for baskets in the nineteenth century. Among the many baskets shown in Anderson's woodcuts were sewing baskets, apple-picking baskets, basket cradles, and large shopping baskets hung on the arm. Berry baskets were usually of willow, but some baskets were made of canoe or paper birch. Early baskets were expensive and probably returnable to the owners.

Baskets were in demand for the marketing of fruits and vegetables all through the nineteenth century. An article in *The Horticulturist, Journal of Rural Art and Rural Taste* of October 1849, gave information about gathering and storing fruit. Peaches, plums, and cherries were gathered in flat-bottomed baskets. Fruit from a dwarf espalier tree was gathered in a common hand basket. In gathering from tall trees a hook was fastened to the handle of the basket, then hung to the tree. When the basket was filled, the fruit was emptied into a larger basket. Apples were also picked in half-bushel baskets, then emptied into bushel-and-a-half baskets for storing. An article on the culture of basket willow in the *Year-Book of Agriculture 1855-1856* provided information about willow baskets and encouraged the growth of osier willow as an American agricultural product. "The willow manufacture in the city of New York is already immense. The amount of imported willow-ware is annually more than three million dollars, while the quantity of unmanufactured willow imported amounts to a much larger sum." The article then discussed the osier willow grown on Staten Island and Newburgh, New York, and tested by different basket manufacturers.

Willow baskets were made on Staten Island as early as 1825 by John Reed. Reed raised his own willow and also furnished willow reeds for New York's many basketmakers. There were also several other basketmakers on Staten Island. In 1840 John Merrill, who raised strawberries and raspberries, made baskets to market them. The baskets in pint and quart sizes were made of black ash with a small handle and marked "J.M." in black. Bushel-size oyster baskets were made of oak and ash. James Morgan made baskets of white oak and maple from 1842 to 1880; some of them are in the Staten Island Historical Society Museum in Richmond, Staten Island.

Nantucket lightship baskets were made aboard the *South Shoal* lightship from 1853 and on the *Cross Rip* ship as early as 1828. Later they were made ashore by retired seamen.

These were splint baskets with ash, white oak, or hickory staves set into pine board bottoms and strengthened by hoops at the top. Many were made with handles and fitted tops, and some old baskets had staves and an encircling weaving of rattan. Nails and tacks were of copper or iron in the old baskets; brass tacks were used later on. Round or oval baskets were made in nests of eight in graduated sizes from one pint to twelve quarts. Many had flat covers. At first the baskets were natural wood finish; later they were varnished. The baskets were used for potatoes, fish, and other commodities, and the larger ones for firewood. The fashionable rattan woven oval baskets with nautical carvings of ebony or ivory were first made about twenty years ago and are still being made.

Splint baskets for fruit were a later invention. In 1859 David Cook of New Haven, Connecticut, made pint and quart splint baskets. The side splints were of basswood, and the bottoms of yellow poplar with round holes for ventilation. L. Wheeler Beecher of Westville, Connecticut, took out a patent for fruit baskets in 1864. The Beecher Veneer Fruit Basket was a round splint basket made in half-pint, pint, and quart sizes. Beecher made a Diamond Basket with side splints of yellow birch crossing to form a diamond pattern. The bottoms were of heavy northern white pine, and the rims were of red oak. Beecher also made Star baskets and square-cornered baskets.

The basket industry flourished. Fruit baskets were produced by William Parry in New Jersey, and round, square, and star baskets were made in Delaware. The Mellish fruit basket, made in New Hampshire about 1862, was shaped like a flowerpot. Square berry baskets were made by the American

Basket Company in New Britain, Connecticut, in 1869. Rochester berry baskets were shaped like round bowls. The baskets made by Old Hibbard Basketwares, South Butler, New York, were of oak, hickory, and elm. In 1876 the Hudson River Basket Depot made square strawberry baskets which were sold with the trade names of Centennial and Eureka. These companies ran advertisements showing cuts of their baskets in the *New England Farmer* and the *American Agriculturist* between the 1860's and the 1880's. The 1880 catalogue of Robert B. Bradley & Company, of New Haven, Connecticut, manufacturer of and wholesale dealer in woodenware and baskets, listed the following kinds of basket: picking baskets handmade: rattan, corn, elm, oak, bamboo with nailed rims; corn or grain baskets: rattan and oak; oyster or clam splint baskets; market baskets, wide splint and rattan; butchers' baskets, bamboo, handles over; grocers' baskets, bamboo, handles at ends; market diamond; laundry, rattan; clothes: oval rattan or oval willow; lunch, fruit, and fancy baskets. And the 1898 Sears, Roebuck & Company catalogue listed: Oak Creek splint corn baskets, tall with handles, three-quarter bushel to two bushels; Racine corn measuring baskets; willow clothes and market baskets; market baskets of woven splint elm; and covered fishing baskets.

The Shakers made and sold a wide variety of baskets and boxes. Utility baskets were made of splint hickory, poplar, ash, or curly maple. Reed palm leaf and rush were used for some smaller baskets, which were round, square, and rectangular, with or without handles and lids. Some baskets were made on a mold. Rectangular-handled carriers, called chip boxes, were used for carrying kindling. Shaker oval boxes of characteristically fine craftsmanship were made of thin bands of maple, one end cut into fingers. The piece was wrapped around a mold and fastened by copper or wrought-iron rivets. The bases of the boxes were of pine. They were sold in nests of graduated sizes. Sometimes the boxes were varnished, and sometimes they were painted red, yellow, orange, or rarer blues or greens. Oval boxes for herbs and pills were early, and round boxes came later. The boxes of the New England colonists were fastened with a vertical lap and wooden pegs; Shaker boxes had finger seams. In addition to small boxes, there were larger butter boxes. The Shaker box industry dates from 1787 to the present. Round boxes were at first made by hand and then, from 1850 on, in factories in Hingham, Massachusetts. Boxes were used on the pantry shelves for cheese, butter, meals, and sugar, as well as for spices. The Shakers also made many boxes for marketing their garden seeds and for the herb industries. Shaker berry boxes were shaped like lopped pyramids with air holes in the sides. The vegetable boxes for kitchen use were similar in shape, but broader and more shallow. The Shakers also carried on a thriving business making bonnets and hats of palm leaves.

The Pennsylvania Dutch made and used many baskets. Their white oak egg baskets were melon-shaped with handles and ranged in size from three inches in diameter to more than two feet. They were also made without handles and tightly woven to hold grain. Similar baskets were made by northern California Indians until the first quarter of the twentieth century. In addition to splint baskets, the Pennsylvania Dutch wove baskets of willow and rye straw. Coiled rye straw bound by oak thongs was also made into beehives and into large hampers with covers for holding dried apples, grain, or feathers. Round Mennonite breadbaskets of coiled rye straw are a popular collector's item. Some have one handle, and an occasional basket has two. There were many other utility baskets made of rye and of willow. Willow and oak wicker-covered bottles, flasks, and large carboys were made throughout the nineteenth century, and the wicker-covered vinegar demijohn is also of that era.

All these baskets, both early and late, are collector's items. Paper, cardboard, and plastics have now replaced baskets as containers for nuts and vegetables, and the paper tote bag is carried by the shopper instead of a basket. Baskets are still made in country districts—especially in Vermont, New Hampshire, and Virginia—but berry and fruit baskets are almost items of the past. Stores of old baskets are often found in attics, in country stores, and in antique shops dealing in country wares. Early baskets were well made and strong. The old wood was carefully seasoned, although constant wear has made splintered edges on the old pieces. Old baskets often have stains which reveal the purpose for which they were originally made.

III

Wrought and Cast Iron

Cast-iron Negro hitching post, eagle door knocker, footscraper, and horse's head hitching post. HENRY FORD MUSEUM.

WROUGHT IRON was the iron which was worked or formed by the blacksmith. Cast iron was poured and cast in a mold at an iron furnace. Both types of ironwork produced interesting articles for the collector of country antiques. Early wrought iron, which included such necessities of Colonial life as nails, latches, and hinges for houses and iron tools and implements, was the work of the blacksmith. He also made handwrought crosses, house numbers, cowbells, and weather vanes. Blacksmiths were among the first settlers to arrive in America. They must have been busy making materials for building, tools for workmen, and hearth and fireplace equipment, such as shovels, forks, pothooks, trammels, and trivets. Builder's hardware included handwrought nails, hinges of various types, hasps, and door latches. Many of these early articles were custom-made for a particular house, and some had names, initials, and dates.

Pennsylvania Dutch hinges and hasps were particularly interesting in design and fine in workmanship. The designs included birds, hearts, such flowers as the tulip, and the types included the H, butterfly, and ram's head hinges. Although the various types of hinges were made in different sections of

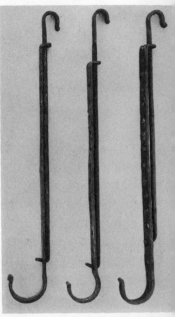

Iron trammels. Late seven-teenth or early eighteenth cen-tury. METROPOLITAN MUSEUM OF ART.

Group of iron cooking utensils. Upper: pie lifter, toaster, and skewers on skewer holder. Lower: pancake turner, fork, and ladle. HENRY FRANCIS DU PONT WINTERTHUR MUSEUM.

Cast-iron pot on legs.
HENRY FORD MUSEUM.

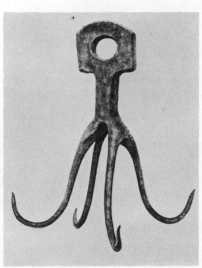

Iron pothook. INDEX OF AMERICAN
DESIGN.

the country, the proportions and finishing touches of the Pennsylvania craftsmen made their products superior to all the others. Much of the iron for the earliest articles was brought from England, but iron foundries had been established in Massachusetts by the middle of the seventeenth century. Until after the Revolution, although several furnaces in New Jersey made camp kettles for the Army, most of the early kitchen utensils were imported from abroad.

Fireplace and kitchen equipment provides one of the largest fields for collecting wrought iron. Articles include spits, hooks, trammels, pokers, toasters, waffle irons, pie lifters, and trivets, as well as shovels, tongs, and andirons. The trammel often held as many as five hooks, from which to hang pots over the open fire. There were also wrought-iron long-handled meat forks, spoons, and ladles and brass strainers with wrought-iron handles. Some of the handles had pierced designs and dates.

Early hollow ware, which included pots, kettles, and spiders (skillets), was of many shapes and sizes. These items had straight sides and flat bottoms, and many had three legs. Although some early pots were made by the blacksmith, most were made on molds at iron furnaces, and as early as the eighteenth century, hollow ware, including pots, skillets, mortars, and kettles of cast iron, were made at furnaces in New York, New Jersey, and Pennsylvania. Iron teakettles, pie pans, stoves, and firebacks were also made. The Shakers at Shirley, Massachusetts, operated a furnace and made their own ironwork.

One category of iron collecting includes the trivets which were set in the fireplace to hold pots. Early trivets were hand-wrought in simple geometric designs and were usually set on legs. Later, they were cast in more elaborate designs, such as the star, heart, swastika, and tulip. In the mid- and late nineteenth century trivets used mainly as stands for irons had even more intricate designs. These included naturalistic flower and leaf motifs and fruits, such as grapes and pineapples. There were also patriotic designs, including the eagle, a cannon and sword, George Washington, the Society of the Cincinnati, and the Lincoln Drape. The G.A.R. Designs representing lodges included the Masons and Odd Fellows, and there was also a Jenny Lind trivet and a Valentine trivet with a design of hearts and cherubs. Late trivets included such mottoes as "Good Luck," and they were also marked with the names of makers. Trivets or sadiron holders were made by all iron companies.

Flatirons, or sadirons, make interesting collector's items. The box iron, with an opening into which a heated slug was inserted, was the forerunner of the familiar flatiron. At the end of the eighteenth century cast flatirons, called sadirons, came into use. Early flatirons were made by the blacksmith and followed no pattern in regard to size or weight. These handwrought flatirons had a variety of decorative handles with fancy curls and twisted forms. Some handles were high, and some had shields to protect the user's hand. Sadirons were larger and thicker than the early flatiron; they were used for smoothing heavy materials. The tailor's smoothing iron was called a goose, and it came in many types and sizes. The commonest goose was the long narrow iron with a pointed tip and square back. A heavy block goose was the earliest type; a smaller goose with a removable handle and long pointed nose came later.

The goffering iron, made as early as the seventeenth cen-

Handwrought iron trivets. INDEX OF AMERICAN DESIGN.

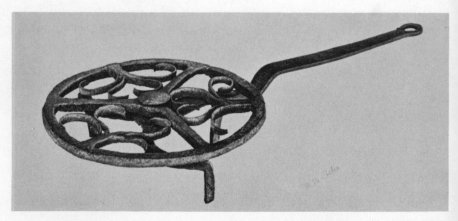

Wrought-iron gridiron. INDEX OF AMERICAN DESIGN.

tury, was the forerunner of crimping and fluting irons. The goffering iron was a fingerlike tube into which a red-hot bar or poker was inserted. It was mounted on a heavy iron standard, which had a tripod base. Often there were two or more tubes of different sizes mounted on a base; one goffering iron had closed tubes heated by a center box which burned charcoal. Crimping and fluting irons were used to crimp and pleat materials. Fluting irons were made in two corrugated sections hinged and locked together. Some fluting irons had a base set on four legs. The base was heated and the cloth to be fluted laid on it, while the second section was pressed down and rocked or rolled to make the fluting. The Knox fluting iron was patented in 1870. Its rollers were on a stand fastened to a heavy rectangular base, which was decorated and held a framed photograph of Susan A. Knox.

Early irons had no marks, but later ones were marked with patents, dates, and weights. Patented irons came in many styles. In 1867 an iron with an upper part made of soapstone, a screwed-on iron handle, and a flat, iron base was patented by Hood. By the middle of the nineteenth century there were many patented irons, including charcoal-burning irons, irons with a font to hold oil for burning, and gas irons. There were also small irons with wooden handles which locked on with an iron clasp. Several could be heated on the stove at once, and a single handle could be moved from one to the other. There were also small irons for traveling and special irons with long points for ironing sleeves. Various types of holders were made for heating one or more irons. A cone holder sat over the open flame and held three irons to be heated simultaneously. A cast-iron tray for the same purpose was patented by Wheeler and Bailey, Utica, New York, in 1862. Irons for

Tailor's goose and shears. INDEX OF
AMERICAN DESIGN.

Crimping iron. About 1866. IND
OF AMERICAN DESIGN.

Box iron with slug.
INDEX OF AMERICAN
DESIGN.

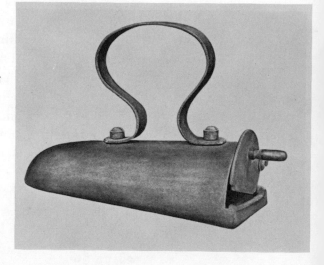

children or manufacturer's models were of various sizes and types, and these make an interesting collection. Some had their own stands. One attractive miniature iron was in the form of a duck.

There are many other late-nineteenth-century cast-iron items for the collector, such as furniture, picture and mirror frames, match and toothpick holders, and children's toys, which include the popular and expensive mechanical banks. Such architectural items as railings, balconies, snowbirds, footscrapers, hitching posts, cast-iron dogs and deer for the lawn, and vases for growing plants were popular Victoriana. Owners of country houses will also be interested in weather vanes. Early wrought-iron weather vanes were in the forms of roosters, eagles, ships, fish, and horses.

One of the specialized cast-iron items is the insurance emblem which was attached to the outside of a building to indicate what company insured the property. Some of these fire marks were lead or tin, but the majority were cast iron. The custom started in Philadelphia in the mid-eighteenth century. The crossed-hands plaque dates from 1752, the Mutual Assurance Company tree from 1784, while the eagle-in-oval mark of the Insurance Company of North America was first issued in 1792. The use of fire marks continued until the end of the nineteenth century. An old-fashioned fire engine was on the United Fireman's Insurance Company emblem of 1860, and an engine also decorated the emblem of the Fireman's Insurance Company of Baltimore, Maryland, which was in business from 1825 to 1904. Other emblems were stars and a man with a fireman's trumpet.

Early prickets to hold candles were made of handwrought iron. These were set on holders to fasten on the wall or to

Fire Department Insurance sign. INDEX OF AMERICAN DESIGN.

Hessian soldiers, andirons. Eighteenth century. METROPOLITAN MUSEUM OF ART.

Smokers' andirons. Eighteenth centv METROPOLITAN MUSEUM OF ART.

Early iron grease, or slut, lamps. HENRY FORD MU-SEUM.

Iron Betty lamp. Seventeenth century. METROPOLI-TAN MUSEUM OF ART.

Stand for rush-light. Seventeenth century. METRO-POLITAN MUSEUM OF ART.

carry as a staff, and some sat on tripod legs on the floor or on the table. There were also sheet-iron table candlesticks, and these continued to be made in the nineteenth century. These late iron candlesticks usually had round bases and stems, with a spring slide to adjust the height of the candle or expel the stump. These were the simple farmhouse candlestick, and they are often found today. A few iron candlesticks had cast-iron bases, usually square. There were also wrought-iron standards which held two or more candles and stood on tripod legs.

Grease, or slut, lamps were used by the early colonists and later in frontier regions. The open reservoir had a wick and a pivoted cover, and the lamp usually hung from a chain. Variations of the grease lamp were called Betty lamps, and late ones sometimes bore the manufacturer's name. There were both iron and tin Betty lamps, and grease lamps were also made in pottery.

Larger collector's items include stoves and firebacks. From early times a large flatiron plate was placed against the fireplace wall partly to increase the heat and partly to serve as decoration. Firebacks were cast in conventional designs, floral motifs, and patriotic, religious, and armorial designs, such as George Washington on horseback and Abraham and Isaac. Andirons were also cast in figures of George Washington, Hessian soldiers, Adam and Eve, busts of women, ships, houses, and Gothic fretwork designs. Earlier handwrought andirons were simple shafts, with ball tips or finials of iron or sometimes of brass.

Many collectors are interested in bells. There are numerous types of small bells, including sleigh bells, Conestoga wagon bells, dinner bells, tea bells, desk bells, handbells, cow-

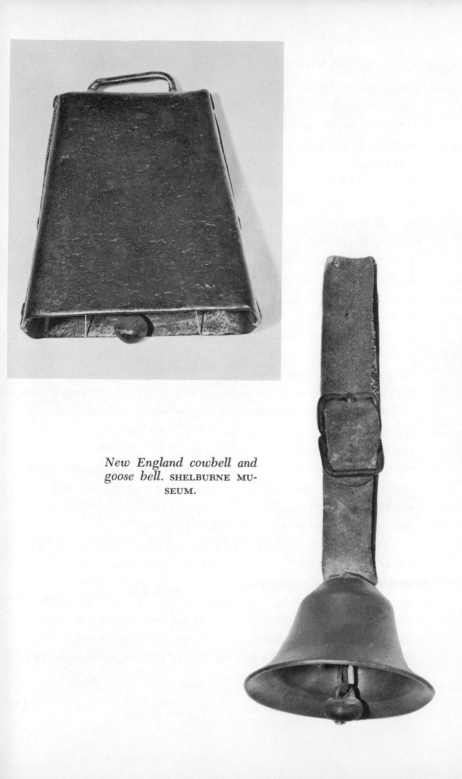

New England cowbell and goose bell. SHELBURNE MU-SEUM.

bells, sheep bells, and turkey bells. Early bells were hand-wrought by blacksmiths, but bells have been made in factories since the early nineteenth century. The bells were of different sizes and shapes and were made of steel, bronze, brass, and sometimes of wood. Sleigh bells, in groups of five, seven, or more small bells, were fastened to a leather strap, which formed part of the harness. Conestoga wagon bells were attached to a wrought-iron frame which held three bells and was fastened to the bridle. The 1891 catalogue of the East Hampton Bell Company (Bevin Brothers Manufacturing Company) showed other types of bells attached to brass shafts, such as horsecar bells, bells for teams of horses, and saddle bells with small bells attached to a center bell which was upheld by a brass shaft.

One bell design, called Eastlake, was built of three angular sections and was made as a single handbell. A group of three was also put on a brass shaft. A chime handbell had bells attached to a circular brass platform, with a wooden handle in the center, used to ring the bell. The school handbell also had a wooden handle. Call bells or desk bells, usually made of nickel-plated steel with a base of metal or sometimes marble, were used on the office desk and on the school-teacher's desk as well. There were larger bells used on rail-road engines, on ships, and on fire engines.

The bells which are true country antiques are those which were used on the farm. The dinner bell hung outside the farmhouse door to call the farmhands to meals. A bell at the barn door rang for special emergencies, such as a fire. Then there were small bells for cows, sheep, and turkeys. Cowbells have been used for many centuries and are in use today. The farmer claims that cows like bells and give more milk if the bells are musical. Cowbells came in several different sizes and were usually made of sheet metal. Clappers were of metal or bone. There were several different types of American cowbells; most popular were the Holstein bells made by the Blum Manufacturing Company. Since the company is now out of business, these bells are worth searching for, especially those that bear their original paper labels. They should be found in old country stores in the Middle West. Long-distance and Kentucky cowbells, made of one piece of steel with a copper finish, have been produced by Bevin Brothers Manufacturing Co. of East Hampton, Connecticut, since 1832. Long-distance bells have spreading sides; Kentucky bells are taller with vertical sides. Hereford bells have also been made for many years. One collector owns a Hereford bell forty years old. Hereford bells are now made by M. & M. Manufacturing Company, Yoakum, Texas. The Hoosier Belle is no longer made because the Riverside Bells Company that manufactured them is out of business. The typical New England cowbell was made of sheet metal dipped in brass and had a riveted vertical side.

Sheep bells were similar to but smaller than cowbells. The small turkey bells were of several types—open cowbell shape, Liberty bell shape, and closed sleigh bell shape. They were made in polished brass and steel with a copper or nickel finish.

Tools: The tools and implements of early American industries, especially those of crafts and occupations no longer in existence, are of interest to many collectors. A few years ago only a small group of specialists assembled such collections as those found at Greenfield Village, Dearborn, Michigan; Old

Museum Village, Smiths Cove, New York; Old Sturbridge Village, Sturbridge, Massachusetts; Shelburne Museum, Shelburne, Vermont and Williamsburg, Virginia, and in the Smithsonian Institution, Washington, D.C.; but now the private collectors number in the thousands. The scope of tool collecting extends from the lathe of the early woodturner and the tools of the carpenter, shoemaker, blacksmith, coppersmith, and silversmith to the larger and more complicated farm implements and mechanical devices. Storage space and interest will help the collector determine what to collect. The tools related to homespun or household activities are personal and seem to appeal to the individual collector, whereas the tools of the farm and village industries suggest collections of larger proportions and more general interest. Since most tools are a combination of wood and metal, the items are valued by both the collector of woodenware and the collector of iron and other metals.

Early tools were made by hand and were simple in design, and their handicraft has great appeal to the collector of country antiques. The tools of the blacksmith, carpenter, tinsmith, builder, shoemaker, and other artisans have a primitive quality that relates them to country living, and these tools of early craftsmen provide insight into pioneer life in log cabins and hamlets. In addition, the collector of country antiques may want to study the simple workmanship and the native woods used in many of the tools.

The earliest tools of interest to collectors were the tools of the pewterer, silversmith, shoemaker, harness maker, carpenter, woodturner, ironworker, and gunsmith. As time went on, other groups of workers came into existence. With the advancement of the cart and wagon, wheelwrights became

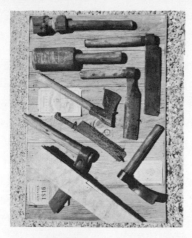

Froes and other splitting tools. PLACE-
MENT BY ERIC SLOANE.

Early American hatchets. PLACEMENT
BY ERIC SLOANE.

Shaker planes for woodworking. INDEX OF AMERICAN DESIGN.

important. Coachmakers and wagonmakers were skilled workmen. The iron and wooden parts of coaches and wagons especially of the Conestoga wagon, called out skilled workmen whose products are treasured today. Along with the introduction of brass and iron foundries came the patternmaker, who made a wooden pattern for each object to be cast in metal. And so through the years a line of expert craftsmen appeared to evolve the needed tools for each new trade. Every trade had its special tools, with blades, hammerheads, and handles each designed for a particular job.

There were dozens of different hammerheads with varying handle lengths, ranging from the delicate upholsterer's hammer to the large blacksmith's hammer and to the claw hammer. There were also many types and sizes of augers. Shears included fuller's shears with long blades, tailor's shears, tin snips, and the glassblower's neck-forming shears. Adzes, which date from the mid-seventeenth century, were made by hand until about 1840. This tool was used by the carpenter and made in a great variety of patterns from the long-handled gutter adz to the short-handled adz used in building post and rail fences. Carpenter's planes and saws formed a long list. The antique wooden planes were made of a combination of rosewood, applewood, and boxwood. The mellow patina of the old wood, together with the fine proportions, make woodworking planes an attractive collector's item. Some were dated and initialed, and others had scallop decoration. There were rabbet planes, molding planes, and bench, or smoothing, planes. Each branch of woodworking had its own planes; the carriage maker, the chairmaker, and the stairbuilder each had his special planes. The late planes had decorative cast-iron handles. There was also a wide variety of saws, ranging from large frame saws to small cabinetmaker's fine dovetail saws and graceful trenching saws made to cut the sides of the grooves for stair treads. Chisels, gouges, and boring tools are another group of tools for the collector.

Dividers and calipers constitute a very interesting class of tools. A divider is a tool used by woodworkers for scribing and measuring. Made of both wood and metal, they often have decorative interest and graceful lines and proportions. There were crude dividers made of such wood as hickory or cherry, handmade metal dividers, and later factory-made metal dividers. Calipers used for measuring thickness of wood or metal, were made in both wood and metal.

The cobbler's bench has become a popular cocktail table for the country house. The old ones were usually made of pine with a tray to hold nails and toolheads, heads, a seat for the cobbler, and a drawer for tools. More elaborate types had extra drawers set within an upright frame at the end of the bench. A small collection of tools used by the shoemaker—awls, hafts, punches, pinchers, sole knives, and hammers—may be displayed on an old cobbler's bench, to become an integral part of the house furnishings and decoration.

A comprehensive collection of tools usually starts with the tools of the first settlers and extends up to the time when the tools became obsolete and were no longer made. What is of prime importance is whether the tool has been superseded. Fine handworkmanship is also of special interest. However, many collections include the later mechanical application of simple tools to machines. The shapes of early tools varied little from century to century since the old tools were designed to do an efficient job. Even some of the later factory-made tools were patterned after the old shapes. There were also the tools and utensils used by the housewife in her various occupations as a spinner and weaver of materials, as a butter and cheese maker, and as a cook. Many of these tools are late and were machine-made, but if they are no longer made, they have historic interest. Even such a humble common article as the potato masher has many forms in different materials—wood, tin, and wire—all now almost obsolete since potatoes are now sold already mashed.

Tools are found in old barns, and many old houses still have their original hardware intact. They may also be found at country auctions and in secondhand shops. Secondhand household utensils are carried by thrift shops, but the early and more valuable tools are now for sale in many antique shops. Magazines and catalogues that picture old tools are also of value to the collector.

IV

Copper and Brass

Brass and copper utensils in home of James Melton. COURTESY
McCall's Magazine.

ADVERTISEMENTS of early makers of copper and brass household utensils in American newspapers date from the early eighteenth century. However, the copper weather vane on the Dutch Reformed Church in Albany, New York, was made in 1656. Henry Shrimpton was said to be working as a coppersmith in New England in 1665, and Caspar Wistar was hammering brass and copper kettles and casting brass buttons in Philadelphia. There were also coppersmiths and braziers in eighteenth-century Boston, New York, Philadelphia, Providence, Annapolis, and such small townships as Bound Brook, New Jersey.

William Bailey, coppersmith, of York, Pennsylvania, operated branch shops in Chambersburg, Hager's-Town, and Fredericktown. According to his advertisement in the Carlisle *Gazette*, July 23, 1792, he made "Stills of all sizes, Brewing coppers, Wash, Fish, and Tea Kettles, Sauce Pans, Coffee and Chocolate Potts." Saucepans stamped with Bailey's name have been found. William Heyser was another Chambersburg coppersmith, and a rare teakettle with a flaring gooseneck and swinging handle is marked "W. Heyser Chambersburg 1825." There are other teakettles of this type stamped with makers' names.

Articles mentioned in coppersmiths' newspaper advertisements included skillets, kettles, coffeepots, teakettles, stew-

Brass stencil for marking boxes.
MR. AND MRS. WILLIAM VERNON
ASHLEY II.

Copper measure. About 1864.
NEW YORK HISTORICAL SOCIETY.

*Turk's-head copper cake pan. Lancaster, Pennsylvania,
about 1835.* INDEX OF AMERICAN DESIGN.

Brass skimmer. HENRY FRAN-
CIS DU PONT WINTERTHUR
MUSEUM.

*Copper skimmer. Late
eighteenth century.*
NEW YORK HISTORICAL
SOCIETY.

*Copper ladle with
wooden handle.* OLD
STURBRIDGE VILLAGE.

pans, baking pans, fish kettles, cake molds, ladles, funnels, and skimmers. Copper utensils were both hammered and cast. Early pieces were hammered out of sheet copper over a wooden mold with a wooden hammer. Spouts and handles were then riveted on pans, kettles, ladles, skimmers, and dippers. The bottoms of old kettles were separate pieces cut in a pattern of tooth edges that joined to the kettle's sides. Old copper is identified by the hand riveting, hammer marks, and irregularities of shape. Some pieces had handles of hand-wrought iron.

There were many coppersmiths in Pennsylvania, and two of their most popular products were copper stills and apple-butter kettles. Stills in rural Pennsylvania supplied Philadelphia and Baltimore with whiskey, peach brandy, and applejack. Most of the old copper stills had fine riveting and planished surfaces. Apple-butter kettles were large open kettles bound with iron. They usually ranged in size from ten gallons to thirty gallons, but "a large copper kettle which holds 250 gallons" and "a brew kettle 300 lbs. weight [which] will contain near nine barrels" were advertised in the *New Jersey Journal* in 1779. Most of the apple-butter kettles used in Pennsylvania during the nineteenth century were made at the Diller Copper Kettle Works in Lancaster. From there they were distributed throughout the country.

An attractive item for collectors of copper and brass is the warming pan. The pans usually combined copper sides and bottom with a cover of brass, and their most interesting feature was the engraved and pierced pattern on the cover. The designs included geometric motifs, flowers, birds, and animals; the tulip was a favorite motif used on warming pans made in Pennsylvania. Engraving these pans required a special workman. Joseph Heddel advertised in a New York paper of 1752 that he engraved copper and brass. Handles were of handwrought iron or of such woods as applewood, ash, and oak. Warming pans were advertised in American newspapers in the early eighteenth century. Paul Revere & Son made and marked warming pans, and William C. Hunneman (1769–1856), an apprentice of Revere's, who operated foundries in Boston and Roxbury, made warming pans, as well as andirons, skillets, kettles, and candlesticks. Braziers and brass founders made warming pans, fenders, door knockers, candlesticks, snuffers and trays, andirons, fire shovels, tongs, coal scuttles, pitchers, milk cans, measures, mortars, and bells. Brass kettles "from a barrel to a quart" were sold in nests. Small copper articles included dippers, strainers, ladles, and tobacco boxes.

The copper kettle is a popular item with collectors. However, so many are now imported from Great Britain and the Continent that the collector should know the characteristics of the American copper kettle in order to identify it. The best way to determine the origin of a copper teakettle is the maker's name on the handle. Comparatively few kettles are marked. When marked, the name usually appears on the top side of the handle. Eighteenth-century makers' names were made with intaglio dies of steel with the lettering cut in reverse. In the late eighteenth and early nineteenth centuries the craftsmen used separate dies of block letters. The impression made by the individual letters was usually deeper than that made by the intaglio die. Some coppersmiths used the name of their town, their street address, and the capacity of the kettle, as well as their name.

Another way to identify an American-made kettle is by its stylistic differences. Although the American teakettle shows the influence of British, Dutch, and Scandinavian copper-

Brass warming pans. Seventeenth century. METROPOLITAN MUSEUM OF ART.

Brass warming pan and shovels. Late eighteenth century. METROPOLITAN MUSEUM OF ART.

Copper coffeepot. INDEX OF AMERICAN DESIGN.

Copper teakettle. Eighteenth century.
INDEX OF AMERICAN DESIGN.

Copper pot with legs. INDEX OF
AMERICAN DESIGN.

opper kettle made in Deerfield,
assachusetts. Nineteenth century.
INDEX OF AMERICAN DESIGN.

Copper kettles. Pennsylvania, nine-
teenth century. LANDIS VALLEY
MUSEUM.

smiths, it has certain different characteristics. The American teakettle may be distinguished by its flared body, tapering gooseneck spout, and dovetailed joinings. Handle shapes varied; some were rounded on the top, others flattened, while still others were bent in a cloverleaf pattern. Teakettles from Britain usually have brass handles those from Scandinavian countries have flat handles. The lid of the American kettle was usually a flat ellipse with a simple finial. American copper kettles were made in sizes ranging from a pint to two gallons. Most American teakettles were made in the East, but they were also produced in New England, the South, and Ohio.

Early brass articles were made of sheet brass hammered over a mold. The handles were riveted on. Sometimes they were handwrought in designs of hearts, tulips, or ovals. In the mid-nineteenth century kettles were made of spun brass. Such articles as measures, funnels, frying pans, pots, foot warmers, and coal buckets were also made of sheet brass. Andirons, candlesticks, door knockers, and furniture mounts were usually cast. Brass candlesticks followed the forms of English candlesticks. The ones that are readily available had baluster stems with groupings of various sizes and shapes of knobs and moldings. Grease trays on early candlesticks were at the base or halfway up the stem, and it was not until the middle of the eighteenth century that they were moved to the socket lip. Nineteenth-century brass candlesticks had heavy, round, or cone-shaped knobs and usually square or rectangular bases. Old brass has a silky surface, and the detail of moldings or beading is more refined than that on later articles. A matched pair of old candlesticks is hard to find. Candlesticks are seldom marked, and often only one of a pair is marked. These nineteenth-century candlesticks are hollow and lighter than early candlesticks since old brass is usually heavier.

American Bellows: Bellows were made by the white cooper in eighteenth-century America and were decorated with turning or stenciled in colors. The earliest American bellows that we have record of were made by Paul Revere. They were made of turned wood and leather, with a brass end. Samuel McIntire, the wood-carver of Salem, Massachusetts, also made bellows. A bill dated November 6, 1808, shows that McIntire was paid twenty-four shillings for carving a pair of bellows for Jacob Sanderson, the cabinetmaker. A pair of mahogany bellows carved by McIntire is in the collection of Mrs. J. Insley Blair; the design is of a basket of flowers with swags and a wreath of roses. McIntire's son also carved bellows. In 1811 there was a bellows-manufacturing company in Albany, New York, and Charles McMurtry patented bellows that were sold in Connecticut and Massachusetts. In 1820 Eckstein & Richardson had a patent for bellows, which were decorated with a painting of a woman and a basket of flowers on one side and a landscape on the other. The bellows illustrated in their advertisement in *Paxton's Philadelphia Annual Advertiser,* 1819, had a medallion of a bunch of grapes as decoration. Their patent was for "Elegant Convex Japanned Parlour Bellows," but they also sold bellows of bird's-eye and curly maple, mahogany, cherry, satinwood, and gum, as well as common bellows of various sizes. The japanned bellows were marked "Eckstein & Richardson Patent No. 36/ Philadelphia."

Bellows were also made of ash and walnut, the latter often carved with leaves or decorated with turning. There are three pairs of bellows in the Metropolitan Museum of Art in New York City; one is walnut, carved with a circular spray of

PHILADELPHIA
Bellows Manufactory.

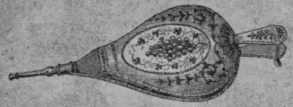

ECKSTEIN & RICHARDSON,

Inform their Friends and the Public that they have on hand a large stock of

COMMON BELLOWS,

OF VARIOUS SIZES;

Bird-eye, Curled Maple, Mahogany, Cherry, Satin-wood and Gum

CHAMBER BELLOWS;

Elegant Convex Japanned Parlour Bellows;

(For which they have obtained Letters Patent.)

And a variety of lower priced Parlour Bellows; all which they will dispose of on the most reasonable terms, at their stores,

36, N. Third St. and 138, Market St.

AND AT THEIR MANUFACTORY,

IN CALLOWHILL, NEAR EIGHTH STREET,

Where they always have on hand Smith Bellows, of any required size, which they will warrant.

JOHN ECKSTEIN,

Respectfully informs his Customers, that he still continues the

BRUSH MANUFACTURING,

In all its various branches, at No. 36, North Third Street, and No. 138, Market Street, and with the addition of the Bellows Business, will be able to give general satisfaction.

Advertisement of Philadelphia Bellows Manufactory. Philadelphia Directory, 1819.

leaves; the plain pair is made of ash and cherry; and the lacquered third pair is decorated with a basket containing a flower and leaves. Bellows were of various shapes—round, rectangular, and the more sophisticated heart shape. Country bellows were usually without decoration. They were homemade of wood and cowhide, decorated with nailheads and braided leather, but they did not have a brass end. This combination of materials makes even the simplest bellows interesting. There were crudely carved bellows made by amateurs, usually women, patterned after designs in books of handiwork, and a design of daisies for painting on bellows was illustrated in the *Art Amateur* for November, 1888.

Bellows found in shops today include those decorated with carving, painting, or stencil designs and simple undecorated country bellows. Most of them were made in the late nineteenth century. Because they have had hard usage, they are not usually in very good condition. However, as an item of country antiques, they are worth collecting, and they are usually inexpensive.

Door Knockers and Powder Flasks: Brass door knockers of the eighteenth century were of shell or vase design. Some had fluting, swags, laurel leaf, and flower motifs. A vase and eagle knocker was popular; it has been reproduced, as have many of the vase designs.

Brass, copper, tin, and zinc powder flasks were made in America from the close of the War of 1812 to the end of the nineteenth century. Early flasks were hand-engraved, but in about 1830 die-stamped metal flasks of brass or copper or a combination of the two metals began to be made. The flasks ranged in size from those holding powder for a small pistol

Plainsman or hunting flask, deer and oak-leaf design.
INDEX OF AMERICAN DESIGN.

Large copper flask with patriotic desi American Flask & Cap Co. About 18
INDEX OF AMERICAN DESIGN.

to those used to supply powder for sporting guns. They also varied in shape, from bottle shapes with long necks to rectangular shapes with short necks and oval flasks with no hips. Flask nozzles, which were made to match the cylinder chambers or bores of guns, also varied. Flasks were made in England and America, but there are enough American flasks for the collector to specialize.

There are three categories of flasks: pocket pistol, military, and sporting flasks. Sporting or hunting flasks seem to relate to country and rural life because of the subject matter of the designs die-stamped on their sides. The designs included dead game, hunting scenes, Indians, deer, dogs, and wickerwork, and there are enough different ones to form a specialized collection. There was a copper flask that depicts running deer and dogs. Another flask had scenes with a dog and rabbit. A design of three ducks in marsh grass within a cartouche was marked "American Flask & Cap Co." Similar designs were also made by James Dixon in England, and the American designs were probably copied from the English. The Bear in Tree flask was made by American Flask & Cap, which also made the Highlander and the Centennial Exposition flasks. A design of an Indian hunter and a deer within a tree border was marked "Batty 1853."

The larger hunting flasks were used in the West, and any large flask could be termed a plains rifle flask. The large overland flasks made by American Flask & Cap had a design of oak leaves enclosing a moose, a hunter and a dog, two dogs, or an Indian rider charging a buffalo. Above the scene was a seven-star chevron and a moose head; below the scene was a small dog or fox head. These flasks were eight inches by four and a half inches and had four round cord rings. Their caps were usually stamped "American Flask & Cap Co."

This design is the most decorative of all the sporting flasks.

A price list of flasks sold by K. K. Tryon Jr. & Co., of Philadelphia, in 1871, included these huntsmen's designs: wreaths, dogs, and birds; wreath and deer; dead game, dog, and tree. An 1881 catalogue of John P. Moore's Sons, New York City, offered: "Heavy fluted, plain." All these designs were patented. The last metal powder flask patent was taken out in 1891.

American makers of power flasks include James Baker, Philadelphia, about 1825; Robert Dingee, New York City, about 1826; Nathan Peabody Ames, Chicopee Falls, Massachusetts, from 1837; John Matthewman, New Haven, Connecticut, 1851 to 1862; John and Joseph Batty, Springfield, Massachusetts, 1846–1860; George Stimpson, 1844; George Adams, 1845; and American Flask & Cap, New York City, 1857–1870.

Perhaps the most common design on flasks was the eagle. Many had an eagle with spread wings, a shield and stars, cannon, and flags and were made especially for the Army. The Peace or Friendship flask had a crest marked "U.S." surrounded by guns and flags, clasped hands within a circle of stars, and an eagle above. The typical Navy flask bore an anchor and the letters *U.S.N.* Many small flasks with eagles were made for Colt pistols. Some of these were marked "Colts Flask." The most interesting ones had an eagle holding a pistol in one claw and a flask in the other. Army and Navy flasks are specialized items, and the serious collector should study the *Powder Flask Book,* by Ray Riling.

Metal powder flasks are not expensive, except for a few rare designs, such as the Batty's Indian hunter, certain Army and Navy flasks, the Centennial flask, and the John H. Hall tin flask, which was used in the Mexican War.

V

Country Pottery

Stoneware pottery. HENRY FORD MUSEUM.

THERE ARE four types of country pottery for the collector: redware, stoneware, brownware or Rockingham, and yellowware. They vary in body, glaze, and decoration, and, to a certain extent, age. The earliest and perhaps most interesting type is redware.

Redware: Redware was a simple, sturdy pottery with a coarse porous texture and crude and colorful decoration. It was made in utilitarian wares in almost every state of the Union from the time of the earliest colonists, but that available to the collector of country wares today came mainly from centers in Pennsylvania, the Shenandoah Valley of Virginia, New Jersey, Vermont and other New England states, Ohio, and Illinois. Country pottery was at first produced in small rural potteries, sometimes operating with a single kiln, but by the mid-nineteenth century some was factory-made. Because the same types of pottery and the same utilitarian shapes were made throughout the years, it is often difficult to tell the early from later pieces.

Redware was made of the same kind of clay as common brick. It had a soft porous body and ranged in color from red-brown to sepia, sometimes showing orange-buff tones. Redware was a folk pottery. It was made by simple farmer potters, and the pieces filled a household need. Besides pie plates, jars, and cooking pots, there were deep vegetable dishes, meat platters, and fancy openwork dishes and trays.

The earliest redware was shaped by hand. When the pieces were dry, they were treated with a glaze, which was either brushed or poured on although a few pieces were dipped in the glaze. The bottoms and bases were left unglazed. This lead glaze was plain for common ware, and colored for the finer pieces, sometimes revealing splotches or streaks of contrasting green or darker brown. After the glaze was applied, the pottery was fired in the kiln. The variations of color of body or glaze were made by the different temperatures of the firing process. Some redware was unglazed, and some was glazed both inside and out. Unglazed redware was shaped into flowerpots, chimney pots, water coolers, hanging baskets, and tobacco pipes. Glazed redware included doorstops, picture frames, and some hanging baskets. In addition, such articles as milk pans, cups, mixing bowls, pie plates, cake molds, and pitchers were glazed inside to protect the food, while the outside was left unglazed.

The forms of redware were simple and utilitarian. One of the earliest was the jar or crock used for storing butter and other everyday commodities. Early redware jars were graceful in shape. They usually had loop handles placed vertically from the rim to the side shoulder or smaller horizontal handles placed on the shoulder of the jar. The neck and base were reinforced and strengthened by a small molding. These jars were made in sizes ranging from one pint up to many gallons and were used for storing apple butter, eggs, sauer-

lipware. Nineteenth century. METRO-
POLITAN MUSEUM OF ART.

Redware with slip decoration in cream
and green. Pennsylvania. METROPOL-
ITAN MUSEUM OF ART.

ipware: sgraffito decoration. Late
ghteenth century. METROPOLITAN
MUSEUM OF ART.

Slipware plate: sgraffito decoration.
METROPOLITAN MUSEUM OF ART.

kraut, and butter. They were made in all localities, and the same shapes were made through the years. The earlier graceful rounded outlines gradually straightened, and solid handles replaced the more easily broken loop handles. Later shapes included the straight-sided butter churn, the common pickle jar with flat pottery lid, the widemouthed butter crock, and the New England bean pot with cover and straight handle. Mugs and pitchers of various sizes and shapes were also made in redware. In Pennsylvania there were redware figures of dogs, lions, doves, peacocks, and horses and riders. Figures were also made at the Bell potteries in the Shenandoah Valley of Virginia.

In addition to glaze, redware could be decorated in two other ways: by slip decoration and by incised line decoration, called sgraffito. Slip-decorated redware, made in America from 1750 to 1900, is one of the most interesting types of country pottery to collect because of its primitive and naïve designs, its mottoes and inscriptions, and the historical allusions of some pieces. Slip decoration was made by tracing designs on the redware shape with a clay of creamy consistency in a contrasting color. The slip was applied to the partially dry ware through a quill or with a slip cup in the same manner in which the present-day pastry cook uses a cake decorator. The dried design was slightly raised above the surface of the body of the ware, but for practical usage was then beaten or pressed into the surface of the plate or platter. The simplest form of slip decoration consisted of lines and dots, but the most interesting pieces are the plates or platters bearing the owner's name, such as "Mary's Dish," names like "Apple Pie," "Mince Pie" and "Shoo Fly," or the name of a national hero, such as Washington. There were also platters

Redware dish decorated in brown, green, and white slip. Pennsylvania, about 1830. INDEX OF AMERICAN DESIGN.

inscribed "Our daily bread" and cookie jars with the owner's initials.

Although much of this slip-decorated redware was made in Pennsylvania Dutch country, it was also popular in New York, New Jersey, Connecticut, Maryland, and Virginia. The commonest type bears inscriptions and designs in yellow slip, but sometimes the slip is in polychrome green, blue, amber, or white. Pieces with names or dates and those with historical significance, such as an eagle or a figure of Washington or Andrew Jackson, are especially interesting and, of course, valuable. Other pieces have mottoes or inscriptions designating them as presentation pieces, such as engagement, wedding, or christening gifts.

The second method of decorating redware was by carving or scratching a design into the body of the piece so that it contrasted with the color of the surface slip when it was dry. This type of redware is called sgraffito ware. Sgraffito decoration was for ornamentation, and it was seldom used on ordinary utilitarian articles. Most sgraffito ware was made in Pennsylvania, and that made in other states was less elaborately decorated. Sgraffito ware was made chiefly for gifts. Decoration included Pennsylvania Dutch inscriptions and traditional motifs from the Old Country, such as birds, flowers, animals, and hearts. The most typical Pennsylvania bird motifs were peacocks, distelfinks, eagles, doves, parrots, pelicans, and barnyard fowl. Among the animals were deer, lions, rabbits, and horses. The flowers included the favorite tulip, lilies, roses, forget-me-nots, and the popular fuchsia, considered sacred because it was one of the first signs of the returning spring. Human figures included spirited horsemen, wedding couples, and women riding sidesaddle. One plate in the Philadelphia

Museum of Art shows a fiddler and two couples dancing. The men wear British uniforms. Around the border of the plate is a German inscription with the date 1786. Many of the inscriptions were biblical quotations, moral sentiments, maxims, and quaint verses. A plate with a design of a dove and tulips has a border which says, "I am very much afraid my naughty daughter will get no man." The names or initials of early potters were inscribed on some plates. Sgraffito ware, usually bearing simple star and cross designs, was also made in Boscawen, New Hampshire. Sgraffito ware was made into the twentieth century, and John Ramsay's *American Potters and Pottery* illustrates a redware pie plate decorated with sgraffito by Jacob Medinger in 1928.

The pieces of redware most available to today's collector are those with simple slip-decorated designs of wavy lines or dots. Pie plates with slip lettering inscriptions of "Apple Pie" or "Lemon Pie" are also not too rare, but any article with the figure of an animal or human or with a date is hard to find and more expensive. Sgraffito ware is much rarer and more expensive than slip-decorated redware, and the signed pieces are particularly expensive. A collection with examples of redware from different sections of the country is interesting; and inscribed or historical figures or a pierced bowl make a unique display for a corner cupboard or the open shelves of a dresser. Pieces from the Bell potteries are also in great demand. Bell pottery was often stamped "John Bell" or "John Bell/Waynesboro." The collector will not find many pieces in prime condition, but plates or platters with small chips are not to be scorned. Unless a piece has a rare maker's name, it is almost impossible to attribute it definitely to one section of the country.

Incised and painted stoneware jug.
METROPOLITAN MUSEUM OF ART.

Painted stoneware jug. METROPOLITAN
MUSEUM OF ART.

Glazed stoneware jug with appliqued
and incised decoration, clasped-hands
design. Ohio. INDEX OF AMERICAN
DESIGN.

Gray stoneware jug, incised an
painted. I. Seymour & Co., Troy, Ne
York, about 1824. NEW YORK HISTOI
ICAL SOCIETY.

In the late nineteenth century molded salt-glazed stoneware, redware and brownware pipe bowls were made at potteries in New Jersey, Pennsylvania, and other localities. Some were fluted, others had raised initials, and still others had a molded head for a bowl.

Stoneware: Stoneware, the second type of American country pottery, came into use about 1800. Stoneware was made from finer clay and was burned at a higher temperature than redware so that it was stronger and less easily broken than redware. Its distinguishing characteristics are its gray to brownish color and its pebbly low-luster glaze made by throwing salt into the hot kiln. Stoneware was mainly made in storage pieces, such as jars, crocks, jugs, and pitchers. There were also plain stoneware fruit jars, churns, pots and pans, pancake batter jugs with spouts for pouring the batter, beer bottles, bean pots, mugs, cups, cake molds, cuspidors, grease lamps, and foot warmers.

Stoneware was decorated chiefly with freehand designs painted in cobalt blue; but some decorated stoneware from Strasburg, Virginia, shows a purple tone, and other decorations are sometimes in brown. The designs include feather scrolls, flowers, and birds, including the eagle, and rare animals and human figures. There are also pieces marked with painted names, initials, and dates. Later some designs were stenciled. Incised line designs were also used and those filled with blue are rare. Modeled decorations could also be applied, and some pieces, including water coolers, vases, jugs, doorstops, and dogs, were made in relief molds. Rare heads, animals, and Toby jugs were modeled by hand. Bird and animal whistles, banks, and miniature pieces were made in all localities early in the nineteenth century.

The finest stoneware clays were found in New Jersey and New York. In New York stoneware was made by the Remmey and Crolius families, who operated stoneware potteries from the early eighteenth century into the mid-nineteenth century. The fifteen potters of the Crolius family ended with Clarkson, Jr., who worked until 1870. A great deal of their stoneware was marked with a stamp, including the name and date. There were many other stoneware makers who stamped their wares. Fine stoneware was also made from the early nineteenth century in Boscawen, New Hampshire, and in Vermont, at St. Johnsbury and Bennington. There were also thriving stoneware centers in Ohio, near East Liverpool and Zanesville, and in Indiana and other Midwestern states. One famous stoneware pottery was owned by the Nortons of Bennington, Vermont, and stoneware was one of the earliest of the famous Bennington wares.

Stoneware, unlike redware, often bears the maker's name and the locale where the piece was made, applied with a stamp impressed in the soft clay. Many pieces also indicated the crock or pitcher's capacity, and often the owner's name was incised or painted on the piece. Stamped stoneware jugs by Remmey and Crolius date from the eighteenth century, and the first known marked stoneware jugs from Bennington were made between 1823 and 1828. When stoneware is not marked, it is almost impossible to identify the maker. The serious collector of stoneware will want marked pieces by well-known potters, as well as pieces from Boscawen, Strasburg, and the potteries of Ohio. Fine Ohio pieces have eagles painted in blue. Molded dog doorstops, foot warmers, and jugs with molded decoration were also made in Ohio. Jugs incised with ships or eagles and the words "Liberty Forever" or with the owner's name are rare, as are water coolers with molded figures of Diana, jugs with horses, pitchers with sprays of flowers, or the clasped-hand jugs made in Ohio. Other sought-after items are animal figures, miniatures, and whistles or banks with animal finials. There are also stoneware jugs with Masonic emblems, Presidential campaign slogans, and presentation jugs. A jug with a deer by a fence and a churn with a long-necked bird are especially interesting, as is a crock with a painted hen and chickens. Late stoneware crocks have stenciled designs, including eagles.

In New York State alone there were more than forty potteries, and potters were also making stoneware in all the New England states, as well as in New Jersey, Pennsylvania, Maryland, Kentucky, and Ohio, with the result that a vast amount of stoneware was produced and a considerable number of old pieces are still on the market. The chief interest in stoneware is in its decoration. The designs were usually incised, painted, or stenciled. Some pieces had no motif but only crude daubs of cobalt blue. The finest pieces were decorated with lively birds, flowers, figures, and animals, and the most coveted decorative motif is the eagle or the American flag or some other patriotic symbol.

The pottery made by the Bell family, of Waynesboro and Strasburg, Virginia, between 1833 and 1899 deserves special mention. It is commonly known as Shenandoah pottery. The Bells made both stoneware and slip-decorated redware. The only decoration was the bright gaudy slip of various colors—olive green, orange red, and manganese brown, resembling

Rockingham. It was usually streaked or mottled. Bell potteries made ordinary baking dishes, pie plates, mugs, jugs, pitchers, washbowls, and soap dishes in redware. After 1852, they also made stoneware articles, including churns, butter jars, crocks, spittoons, figures, hanging flower baskets, and wall flower holders. The Bells evolved many distinctive types, such as picture frames decorated with eagles, candlesticks, figures of dogs, squirrels, birds, geese, and human figures with applied relief decorations. Much of the Bell pottery was marked with the various names of the family and the location impressed in the clay.

Several categories of redware and stoneware collecting would form unique collections. Redware and stoneware banks, whistles, figures, and miniatures are fascinating fields for the specialist. The miniature figures and toys were made principally in Pennsylvania and are, for the most part, crude imitations of Staffordshire earthenware figures. There are various birds, some whistles, and dogs, including reclining poodles and hounds and crude poodles carrying baskets in their mouths. There were also horses, some not unlike the rare English Whieldon horses. There were also lions, deer, peacocks, doves, snakes, and an occasional human figure. These are rare.

Redware and stoneware banks in jug and beehive shapes were made in various potteries, some in cream or gray stoneware with cobalt blue decoration, others with a brown or orange glaze. There were others in the shape of lions, dogs, and books. Miniature pots and tea sets, rare, expensive, and much sought-after by collectors today, were also made at various potteries.

Brownware or Rockingham: Brownware came into use after 1845 and soon took the place of the heavier handmade pottery. Brownware has a light buff body with a solid dark brown or mottled brown glaze. Brownware was made by quantity production methods and was first produced in America by D. & J. Henderson, Jersey City, New Jersey, but it is known as the typical pottery of Bennington. Contrary to general belief, however, all brownware or Rockingham is not Bennington, and large quantities were made in Ohio and many other localities. In fact, East Liverpool, Ohio, produced the great bulk of Rockingham and yellowware made in America between 1840 and 1900.

Although some brownware was handmade on the potter's wheel, most was made in factories and pressed in plaster-of-paris molds. In color, brownware ranged from bright light brown to dull dark brown and black. It was made in ordinary jars, jugs, crocks, pitchers, bottles, milk pans, plates, cups, and mugs, bean pots, and pancake batter jugs. Cake molds, cuspidors, doorstops, and foot warmers were also made in brownware pressed in molds. Many dog doorstops were made in the Middle West, and toys, bird and animal whistles, banks, and miniature pieces were made by hand particularly in the Midwestern potteries.

At Bennington, Rockingham ware was usually pressed in molds. There were jars; spittoons with shell, Gothic, and acanthus panel designs; and pitchers in many patterns, including hound-handled pitchers, paneled pitchers with flowers, and pitchers with grapevine and acanthus-leaf designs pressed in panels. There were also pitchers with hunting scenes made in Rockingham and the lighter flint enamelware. Flint enamel, which had green, brown, yellow, and orange flecks in a bril-

Brown Rockingham Tobies, coachman bottle, dog doorstop, bowl, and pitcher. HENRY FORD MUSEUM.

Brownware soap dishes. BENNINGTON MUSEUM.

Brownware and flint enamel cuspidors—clamshell, panel, and acanthus designs. BENNINGTON MUSEUM.

liant glaze, originated at Bennington in 1850, but was copied
by potteries in Ohio a few years later. Bennington also made
cow creamers; figures of dogs, lions, and deer; Tobies; coachman, and book bottles, and other flasks. Small log cabin and
chest-of-drawers banks are rare.

Household utensils made at Bennington included washbowls and pitchers, soap dishes, shaving mugs, slop jars, chamber pots, footbaths, foot warmers, and bedpans. All these
articles were also made elsewhere, particularly in Ohio. For
the kitchen there were brownware cake, jelly, and pudding
molds, pipkins with covers and handles, pie plates, baking
dishes, mixing bowls, and milk pans.

Tableware included complete tea and coffee sets in heavy
paneled forms and a variety of patterns. The covered bowls
and dishes are rare, but sugar bowls are available. Toddy cups,
mugs, goblets, and teapots are the most popular collector's
items. There were plain paneled teapots, teapots with alter-
nate rib patterns and acanthus-leaf patterns, but contrary to
popular belief, the Rebbeca-at-the-Well teapots were never
made at Bennington. Covered tobacco jars with various
molded patterns, including Gothic arches, were made in both
Rockingham and flint enamelware. Ornamental pieces included picture frames, lamps, candlesticks, figure bottles,
Tobies, curtain tiebacks, and tulip vases copied from the
Sandwich glass celery vase.

Rockingham and flint enamel candlesticks were made in
various baluster forms similar to those of silver and plated
candlesticks. There were also rare chamber candleholders
with saucers and handles in plain or acanthus-leaf patterns.

Novelty items, which are popular with collectors, included
inkwells in the form of lions and hounds, paperweights, desk

sets, book flasks, Toby snuff jars, pitchers, and coachman bottles. Toby snuff jars are rare. They were made at Bennington in several different styles, sizes, materials, and glazes. The hats on all these snuff jars were removable covers. A few Toby snuff jars were marked. Toby bottles were made in Rockingham, flint enamel, and graniteware and were sometimes marked. There were three types, the rarest being the man astride a barrel. Rockingham was rarely marked, and the finest early Rockingham ware is difficult to place when not marked. Ohio copied the Bennington wares, including the hound-handled pitcher, book flasks and picture frames, and the finest Ohio Rockingham is often taken for Bennington. There are some thirty different hound-handled pitchers and many dog doorstops, all made in factories from New Jersey and Vermont to the Middle West. Such articles as candlesticks, curtain knobs, picture frames, goblets, cow creamers, and hound-handled pitchers made at Bennington were not marked. Some articles, such as Toby mugs and jugs, were sometimes, but not often, marked. The quality, brilliance, and color of the glaze will identify fine wares, but not the maker.

Some pieces may be identified by pattern and design. For example, Bennington Toby jugs may be identified by their flat bottom and the grapevine or boot handle. Bennington Tobies included two types of Ben Franklin, a General Stark, and a sitting Toby. The Toby jug made at New Jersey potteries had a Toby head, but the jug was paneled. Hound-handled pitchers may be identified by the position of the hound's head and paws. The nose of the hound on the Bennington hound-handled pitchers touched its paws, leaving a space between the head and the pitcher, whereas the head of the hound on the New Jersey pitchers was free from the pitcher or rested flat against the handle.

For the beginning collector, the best advice is to look for good quality and condition. Leave the object with the maker's name for the experienced collector. The serious collector of Bennington will need Richard Carter Barret's books for reference and will also want to take a trip to the Bennington Museum. Even then an expensive item is best purchased from a well-established antique shop.

Yellowware: Yellowware, finer than pottery but coarser than earthenware, was a transitional ware. Not handmade, it was produced from molds in factories. It was the cheapest and plainest form of earthenware, made by the same methods, of the same clay, and in the same factories as brownware. The clear glaze used on yellowware intensified the buff color of the body. Pieces usually varied from pale buff to deep yellow; but some articles of yellowware were partly brown and cream, and still other articles were yellow with blue or white bands. Yellowware was made in utilitarian pieces and seldom molded or relief-decorated. Little yellowware was made at Bennington, and, as a result, Bennington yellowware is rare. There are, however, a few custard cups, pie plates, and pipkins and a rare yellowware cow creamer and Toby snuff jar, as well as a few standing poodles holding baskets in their mouths.

East Liverpool was the yellowware center in Ohio, but it was also made at Zanesville and Cincinnati and in Pennsylvania. Pieces made in the towns along the Ohio and Mississippi rivers were distributed by boats as far south as New Orleans. It was also peddled from door to door throughout the Middle West.

Redware dish. New Jersey, about 1850. METRO-
POLITAN MUSEUM OF ART.

*Redware pitcher. Strasburg
Virginia, nineteenth century*
METROPOLITAN MUSEUM O
ART.

Yellowware plate and cups. BENNINGTON MUSEUM.

There were plain yellowware jars, pitchers, mugs, cups, plates, bowls, butter, pudding, and jelly molds, soap dishes, teapots, and tureens. Yellowware mugs, pitchers, bowls, and plates were also decorated with blue, black, brown, or white bands. Some pieces resembled kitchen mixing bowls, and some were related to mocha ware. A few pieces of yellowware, such as candlesticks, doorstops, and pitchers, were pressed in the same molds as those used for Rockingham. Yellowware pudding molds with ear-of-corn designs are a favorite with collectors. A rare yellowware mug made in East Liverpool had wavy bands striped with cobalt and manganese and a frog at its bottom. A six-paneled pitcher with a raised floral design was made in Ohio and was marked "W. Bromley & Co., Brighton Pottery, Cin. Ohio." However yellowware was seldom marked, and few pieces can be attributed to a particular factory.

Clay Tobacco Pipes: The oldest pipes made in America were those of the Mound Builders of the Mississippi Valley. They were usually made of carved and polished stone to represent birds, animals, including the bear, turtle, toad, lizard, serpent, and mastodon, as well as some human heads. The pipes were shaped in one curved piece with the bowl rising from the center. Some clay pipes were also made, and the Indians found on the coast when the first white settlers arrived smoked clay pipes. Rudely made of yellow or blue-gray clay, most had simple molded bowls and stems, but some idol pipes had figures of animals or birds. The Onondaga Indians of New York made curved stem pipes with the bowl and stem in one piece; one stem had a bear's head. These date from the seventeenth century. However, as early as 1586 Indian pipes were carried to Europe and served as the models for English and Dutch pipes, which were later exported to America in the seventeenth and eighteenth centuries.

The early-seventeenth-century pipe had a small bowl. Later in the century, when tobacco became cheaper, the pipe bowl became larger. Early English pipe bowls have been found in Revolutionary diggings. Some were marked "TD" on the pipe bowl in a circle and "T or D" on the heel, which held the pipe upright. Other markings included "R Tippet" within a circle on the bowl; still others were marked "W.G." Rare pipes with the British royal arms have also been discovered, as well as Dutch long-stemmed or churchwarden's pipes. Pipes marked "TD" within a circle of thirteen stars have been unearthed in the campsites of the War of 1812. "TD" pipes were made and used well into the twentieth century.

However, according to John Thomas Scharf and Thompson Wescott in their *History of Philadelphia,* tobacco pipes were made in Philadelphia as early as 1690. The earliest advertisement of tobacco pipes made in America appeared in the *American Mercury,* Philadelphia, May 12, 1725: "Good long Tavern Tobacco Pipes sold xxx by Richard Warder Tobacco Pipe Maker." The New York *Gazette,* March 24, 1735, carried an advertisement of a house for sale in Flushing with "about Twenty Acres of Clay ground fit for making tobacco Pipes, with two Negro slaves, utensils and other conveniences to carry on that business."

Pipe making was also an industry of the Moravians in their settlements in Bethlehem, Pennsylvania, during the early nineteenth century. The pipes they made had plain bowls, some of white and some of red clay. Pipe bowls in the form

Clay pipes made at Salem, North Carolina, glazed brownware and unglazed white clay. OLD SALEM.

Molded and plain pipe bowls. Upper: two stoneware, redware unglazed. Lower: molded stoneware with bamboo stem. Dark-brown Rockingham, white clay, head of President Fillmore. Plain unglazed redware. HENRY FORD MUSEUM.

of a man's head were made in potteries in New Berlin, Pennsylvania, from 1810 to 1845. Black glazed pipe bowls were made by country potters and sold in Lancaster, Pennsylvania, in the first half of the nineteenth century. In 1840 Samuel Sturgis had an extensive clay pipe business at Lititz. He made pipe bowls in several designs, glazed in green, brown, or yellow, for sale to tobacconists in Philadelphia and other cities. Another Pennsylvania potter who made clay pipe bowls was John Gibble. His pipe bowls were of red clay, glazed in brown, in the shape of an Indian's head. The Gibble Pottery was in business until the end of the nineteenth century. White clay pipes were made in the Kensington district of Philadelphia in 1858 by potters from England and in Lancaster from 1825 to 1900.

The making of clay pipes was an important industry in the Wachovia Moravian settlement of Old Salem, North Carolina. Because of the excellent deposits of clay, the pottery business there had thrived since the 1750's. An inventory of April 30, 1804, of pottery owned by the Salem congregations listed 200 dozen glazed pipe heads and 4,000 dozen unglazed pipe heads, which were shipped as far north as Philadelphia. The heads of the pipes were of various designs of molded clay, and reeds from nearby streams provided the stems. These pipes were made well into the twentieth century, and the craft is carried on today in the restored Single Brothers House in Old Salem, where visitors may buy pipes made in the old designs.

The Shakers also carried on a pipe-making industry at Niskayuna and Watervliet, New York, in the early nineteenth century. The pipe bowls were of red or white clay, and the long stems were made of willow. From 1837 to 1847 the use of tobacco was prohibited in spirit messages, and the industry temporarily waned.

Clay pipe bowls played an interesting role in several Presidential campaigns. They were molded in likenesses of several Presidents, including Henry Clay, 1832; Millard Fillmore, 1850; Franklin Pierce in the 1850's; James Buchanan, about 1857 to 1861; Abraham Lincoln, about 1860; Andrew Johnson, about 1865; Ulysses S. Grant, about 1869; William Henry Harrison, 1888; Grover Cleveland, 1892; and William Jennings Bryan, 1908. The Fillmore pipe bowl had a molded head of Fillmore with a wreath and the raised words "President" on one side and "Fillmore" on the other. It was made in Pennsylvania. The Buchanan pipe bore a raised figure of a buck on one side of the bowl and a mounted cannon on the other. The bowl of the first Lincoln campaign pipe had a molded design of an eagle with spread wings on one side and a liberty cap with crossed flags on the other. A later Lincoln pipe had a portrait bowl with "A Lincoln" impressed in the stem. The General Grant pipe also had a portrait bowl with "General Grant" impressed in the stem.

These pipes were made by Barney Spring, who worked in Rochester, New York, and in Boston until the 1890's. Spring also made the diminutive pipe with the three Prince of Wales feathers, to commemorate the prince's visit to America in 1860, and the plug-ugly portrait pipes of Tom Sayers, the prizefighter. The bowls of these pipes were molded heads of the fighter. The white clay pipes with the portrait bowls of Harrison and Cleveland were made by Charles Kurth of Brooklyn, New York. In New York in the 1880's A. Peyrau, a Frenchman, was making red unglazed terra-cotta pipe heads of Peter Cooper and other prominent men of the time.

W. F. James made clay pipes which were given away with bags of Moonshine Tobacco in 1910. These were marked "Moonshine" and decorated with a crescent moon.

The old Indian and Mound Builders pipes are available in shops today. They may also be seen in such museums as the Museum of Natural History, in New York City, and the Smithsonian Institution, in Washington, D.C. The New-York Historical Society owns a collection of English, Dutch, and American pipes from diggings in and around New York City, as well as some Presidential pipe bowls. In the 1890's Barney Spring made a set of Presidential pipe bowls for the Smithsonian Institution from the molds and dies he had used years before. They may be seen there today.

Although pipes may still be found in old diggings, the time spent is seldom rewarding. The old pipes, although all handmade, were always cheap, so that they were not valued by their owners. They were made of cheap clays—redware, brownware, yellowware, and stoneware—and their stems were of willow or other reeds. The molds were of wood, lead, or tin. Fine clays for pipe making are found in the Mississippi Valley and in Pennsylvania, Delaware, Virginia, and South Carolina, and in these areas clay pipes were made until the end of the nineteenth century. When clay tobacco pipes were no longer in demand, the companies began making toy pipes for blowing soap bubbles instead. The clay soap bubble pipes have now been replaced by metal pipes, so that even the old bubble pipe is a collector's item today.

Monkey or Slave Jugs: The monkey jug or slave jug is another product of the country potter. In nearly all countries and times, potters have made these jugs, expressing their jests

Grotesque slave jug. Connecticut, nineteenth century. INDEX OF
AMERICAN DESIGN.

Grotesque jug. New York, about 1850. INDEX OF AMERICAN DESIGN.

and jibes in grotesque pottery caricatures. Many such jugs were made in Germany, and in England nineteenth-century Staffordshire jugs bore whimsical figures of national heroes, such as Wellington and Nelson. In America the earliest grotesque jugs were made by the Mound Builders of the Middle West. Grotesque jugs were also made by American Indians, but those that particlarly interest the collector of country antiques were made at the small nineteenth-century American potteries or by country amateurs, such as slaves. These grotesque monkey or slave jugs were made of ordinary clays, such as redware, stoneware, and brownware, both glazed and unglazed, the glaze ranging from olive brown to dark brown or black. They were made to hold liquor, ale, or cider, usually in the form of a cider jug with a handle, a small short neck and a cork stopper.

The jugs showed a crude profile with a large nose. Huge protruding ears sprang from the sides of the jug, and the large round eyes and open mouth with teeth that were sometimes movable suggest a voodoo figure. In fact, the jugs are often called voodoo jugs.

Grotesque jugs were made in various country potteries throughout the United States from New England—Vermont, Massachusetts, and Connecticut—south to Virginia and west to Ohio. Some were made by Negroes on plantations after the Civil War, but others are known to have been produced in well-known potteries. The jugs were sometimes marked with incised names, but there is no information concerning the identity of the person whose name was scratched on the jug. Was he the potter or the person represented in the caricature? No one knows. Most of the jugs date from the middle of the nineteenth century. There are not many available, but there

rease lamp, stoneware. Ohio, about 1850. INDEX OF AMERICAN DESIGN.

Grease lamp with pinched bowl. Ohio. INDEX OF AMERI-CAN DESIGN.

Grease lamp with teapot-shaped bowl. Ohio. INDEX OF AMERICAN DESIGN.

are also few collectors; however, grotesque jugs undeniably make interesting conversation pieces for open country shelves.

Grease Lamps: Another product of the country potter was the grease, or slut, lamp. These were similar to the open-saucer iron and tin lamps and related to the Betty lamp. In fact, some Betty lamps were made of pottery. Grease lamps had an open reservoir on a standard set in a saucer base. The lamp had one or two handles and a beak or spout for a wick rest. Opossum or coon fat often provided the fuel. Grease lamps were made of redware and stoneware. The redware was usually given a dark-brown glaze, but some lamps had a mottled pattern, and those made in Winston-Salem, North Carolina, had a combination of brown, black, and cream or a green slip on a yellow-brown ground. No two grease lamps were alike, but they followed old types made from about 1770 to 1870. Grease lamps ranged in height from three to seven inches and had a stocky shape, with a heavy standard rising from a saucer and bulging into an oval receptacle for grease, which may resemble a teapot. Sometimes the standard was fluted, as in the lamps made in Pennsylvania, and sometimes the grease receptacle was pinched at the top. Some lamps were unusually tall, and others were as short as a chamber candlestick; still others were enlarged saucers without a standard. A unique grease saucer lamp, made by David Spinner of Bucks County, Pennsylvania, between 1800 and 1811, was heart-shaped. Another rare type is a saucer lamp with three spouts. But the rarest grease lamp of all is the small pottery Betty lamp. Grease lamps were made in Pennsylvania; in Morgantown, West Virginia; by the Moravians in Salem, North Carolina; in Tennessee; and in Ohio. More have been found in

Match holder, sewer tile clay. Ohio, 1875–1900. HENRY FORD MUSEUM.

Match holder, sewer tile clay. Ohio, 1875–1900. HENRY FORD MUSEUM.

Pennsylvania than in any other part of the country. Grease lamps are rare. The dates are uncertain, for the old types were made for many years. Grease lamps are also made by present-day potters.

Sewer Tile Pottery: A late product of the potter were the crude animals and match holders made of sewer tile clay. They were probably made after hours by workmen at the tile factories. The Henry Ford Museum has an interesting collection, and pieces are often seen at Midwestern antique shows. The pieces were primitive and whimsical dogs, lions, alligators, eagles, and other animals, some of which resemble the claywork of nursery-school children. Dots and lines cut by a crude tool suggest eyes, noses, mouths, and skins or feathers. There were also match holders made of joints of sewer tile, with hand-molded figures of eagles, frogs, and other animals clasping the pipe. These are attributed to the National Sewer Tile Company of Akron, Ohio. These pieces, all dark brown, were made in Ohio between 1875 and 1900. They present a new item for the collector of small country antiques but so far have only been found in the shops of Midwestern dealers. They are reasonable in price, but the supply may not be plentiful.

VI

Homespun and Handwoven

Home of Mr. and Mrs. Ben Prins, showing hooked rugs with roosters. The
Complete Book of Small Antiques Collecting, BY KATHARINE M. MC CLINTON

MOST OF THE material for early American clothing, bed linens, table linens, curtains, and upholstery was made of the native wool, flax, and cotton spun and woven in almost every Colonial home. The old homecrafted materials have a simplicity and honesty that make them a sincere expression of folk art. Flax and wool were raised by the early settler, but the lengthy process of cleaning, hackling, and sorting the flax, as well as the final spinning and weaving, was the job of the housewife. Quantities of linen thread were woven into sheets and tablecloths. Fustians and striped dimities were also made. The linen was usually plain textured, but there were decorative checked patterns of blue and white as well. Woolens were also woven in blue-and-white checked designs for blankets, carpets, and dress goods.

The women of the household also did the dyeing of materials. Indigo blue and cochineal dyes could be purchased, but many housewives brewed their own dyes from native woods, roots, and flowers. They followed the early books of instruction for weaving and dyeing, which also included various patterns. "A Treatise on Weaving, Consisting of near 300 different Draughts, with full and plain Directions of the Preparations of the Yarn, Warping, and Weaving of Barrogan, Tammy, Durant, Paragon, Duroys, Serge denini, Grogram. By David Valentine of Suffolk County, Long Island" was advertised in the New York *Gazette or the Weekly Post-Boy,* January 6, 1772. In addition to cochineal, red and scarlet could be brewed from camwood and pokeberry roots. Blue came from larkspur flowers, purslane, wax myrtle, and spiderwort; yellow from coreopsis flowers, turmeric, sumac, osage orange, alder, birch, walnut, hickory, and from the bark of yellow oak; green could be produced from combinations of blues and yellows. Browns came from the bark of oak, walnut, maple, hemlock and butternut; blacks, from logwood and field sorrel. The dahlia was used to dye wool orange, and zinnias produced yellow.

Newspaper advertisements reveal the existence of numerous professional weavers in America in the eighteenth century. There were journeymen weavers: "upwards of 100 Journeyman weavers have engaged to go to New York and Boston where they are promised constant employment," reported a news item from London in the New York *Gazette or the Weekly Post-Boy,* on February 1, 1768. There was a linen manufactory in Boston in 1765 that made "Bengals, Lillepusias, and Broglios," and there was a woolen manufactory on Chapel Street in New York City in 1769. The St. Andrews Society of New York employed "poor Scots women" to spin flax, wool, or cotton for the merchants David Shaw and David Milligan in 1762. Family weaving was also encouraged by various colonies and by prizes given by the Society for Promoting the Arts, and many families wove both woolens and linens of their own raising. In Woodbridge, New Jersey, the family of "Mr. Isaac Freeman wove 599 yards, Mr. James Smith, 567 yards and Mr. Nathaniel Heard 414 yards," according to the New York *Gazette or the Weekly Post Boy*, January 18, 1768. Similar advertisements refer to family weaving in Newport, Rhode Island; Lancaster, Pennsylvania; and Fairfield, Connecticut.

Among the various items of early handweaving, the woven coverlet interests the collector more than any other pioneer textile. Woven coverlets, either made by a housewife who spun, dyed, and wove the material or by a professional weaver, were produced in America during the eighteenth and all through the nineteenth century. The housewife spun the flax and the wool for weaving the coverlets, the patterns were handed down by tradition and came to America from the European homeland.

Coverlets were made with several types of weaving technique, including overshot, summer and winter, and Jacquard weaves. The overshot weave was a favorite of workers on the early handlooms. It was a loose weave of wool weft on a linen or cotton warp. The coverlets on linen warp usually date from the eighteenth century. Overshot coverlets were made in simple geometric patterns, but the names were picturesque and reflected the social and historical events of the time; they included Indian Trouble, Federal Knot, Downfall of Paris, and Jackson's Purchase. Others, such as Church Windows, Wheel of Fortune, Rose in the Bush, and Blazing Star, bore a faint resemblance to familiar objects. These coverlets were patterned in shades of blue, red, brown, rust, rose, black, brown and tan, and yellow and green. Scarlet obtained from cochineal was rare. Coverlets made on home looms were made of two lengths sewed together, thus possessing a center seam.

Coverlet, overshot weave, wool and cotton. Early nineteenth century. INDEX OF AMERICAN DESIGN.

Woven coverlet, hand-spun wool and cotton, vegetable dyes. Kentucky, about 1847. INDEX OF AMERICAN DESIGN.

Overshot weave coverlets were made in all the colonies and by the Western settlers. Those still available usually date from the nineteenth century.

Summer and winter is a double weave. The most common coverlets made in this weave were usually blue and white in a reversible geometric pattern—white for summer and blue for winter. They were also made in rose and rust. Most of these coverlets were woven in New York and Pennsylvania, and they date from the first third of the nineteenth century. It was also at about this time that the first Jacquard coverlets were made in America.

The Jacquard loom was an invention of the nineteenth-century industrial age that revolutionized the weaving industry. Its inventor was a Frenchman, Joseph Marie Jacquard. The Jacquard coverlet was woven by a professional weaver because the loom required a skilled operator to follow the intricate patterns. Many of the elaborate patterns woven on the Jacquard loom are not as interesting as the older, less sophisticated designs. The most common had a center medallion with borders of scrolls, festoons, flowers, birds, and trees. Rarer coverlets depicted buildings, ships, Masonic emblems, eagles, and patriotic figures, such as George Washington. Some included mottoes. Often the name of the weaver or the person for whom the coverlet was made and the date and place of its creation were woven into one corner.

An early coverlet with a border of eagles and Masonic emblems was woven by Joseph Youngs, and dated September 4, 1822. It is in the collection of the Old Museum Village of Smith's Cove, in Monroe, New York. A similar coverlet bore the inscription "Agriculture and Manufacturers are the Foundation of our Independence." A coverlet woven in Ohio

Boston Town. Blue and white wool and linen Jacquard double weave coverlet, 1850. HENRY FORD MUSEUM.

"The Hemfield Railroad." Jacquard coverlet, dark blue and white. SMITHSONIAN INSTITUTION.

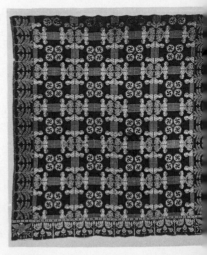

Campaign coverlet, General Zach Taylor. Indigo blue wool and wh cotton. Maryland, 1847. SMITHSON INSTITUTION.

in 1842 had a design of birds and flowers, with the following verse woven into the corners:

> Be ye to others kind and true
> As you'd have others be to you
> And neither say or do to them
> What e'er you would not take again.

The well-known Boston Town pattern had a grape border, many buildings including Chinese temples, and a variety of sailing vessels in the harbor. It was woven in 1850, probably in New England, and one is now in the Henry Ford Museum. Other coverlet borders were Tree and Eagles, Bird and House, Picket Fence and Oak Tree, and Chanticleer. A campaign coverlet inscribed with "General Zachary Taylor, Rough and Ready" and bearing a tree border was woven in 1847, and in 1851 a coverlet, "The Hemfield Railroad," was woven in West Virginia to commemorate the building of the railroad. Another coverlet has an all-over design and border of pairs of animals that suggest Noah's ark.

Many Jacquard coverlets were woven in Pennsylvania. Certain motifs, including the heart, star, peacock, turkey, and rooster, are typically Pennsylvania Dutch, but some Pennsylvania coverlets also feature the rose, eagle, house, and patriotic motifs. Pennsylvania coverlets are favorites with collectors. However, coverlet weaving was not confined to one locale but was universally practiced from north to south and to the west. Patterns seem to have been common property, but certain well-known designs were popular in different regions. Patterns were doubtless passed from one housewife to another, but the itinerant weavers probably had pattern books. One such pattern book, the "Draft Book," belonging to John Landes in the late eighteenth century, is in the Philadelphia Museum of Art. It shows patterns marked off in squares, so clearly that they could be followed by present-day weavers. But even until the Civil War the majority of the women in remote districts did their own weaving, and on many Southern plantations there were loom rooms or weaving sheds, where a slave spent most of her time at the loom. Coverlets were made in New York, Ohio, Indiana, and Kentucky in the 1830's and 1840's, and they were woven well into the 1870's. The span of years during which the Jacquard coverlet was popular renders it a product of Victorian America.

Many of these old coverlets are found in excellent condition, today except for the fringe. Because the fringe was made separately and attached after the coverlet was woven, it can be removed and replaced by fringe from another old coverlet, or it can be used only on the sides, leaving both the top and the bottom without fringe. A great number of coverlets have the maker's name woven in the corner. Thus, there are records of the names of many makers, including the well-known Sarah La Tournette, of Indiana, who worked in the 1850's. Guy F. Reinert in his booklet, "Coverlets of the Pennsylvania Germans" lists almost eighty Pennsylvania weavers, and more are being discovered. The earliest dated American Jacquard loom coverlet made in Pennsylvania bears the date 1831, but one dated 1821 has been found in New York State. Not all coverlets were dated. Jacquard coverlets were made in both single and double weaves, usually in one width without a center seam. The earliest coverlets were in double weave and usually restrained in design. Later ones, especially those made in the Middle West, were in single weave. The colors most commonly used were red, blue, and white, but green, pink, saffron yellow, and other shades were sometimes chosen. Vegetable dyes produced clear and vivid hues. The rarest coverlets had borders with eagles or other birds, houses, or figures. Coverlets with center designs of houses, such as the Boston Town design, Chinese pagodas, and sailing ships and the red, white, and blue coverlet with pairs of animals are particularly interesting and rare.

The work of the independent weaver was later supplemented by the products of spinning and weaving mills. There a few mid-nineteenth-century tablecloths were also woven in designs similar to those of the coverlets.

Handmade Country Rugs: The first floor coverings of early America were probably rag rugs made out of scraps of old materials. However, there were woven carpets made by professional weavers. Joseph Cherry advertised "carpeting of all kinds from the highest to the lowest degree" in the New York *Herald,* October 26, 1796. Thomas Thompson of Goshen, New York, advertised "weaving of carpets" in the Goshen *Repository,* June 13, 1797. In most early American houses, however, the floor coverings were made by the housewife. The bed and table rugs of the Connecticut River Valley, dating from the early 1700's, show the technique of some of these early-eighteenth-century rugmakers. These were wool embroidered on a wool background, the entire surface covered with a deep uncut pile. The designs, including the Tree of Life, were similar to those of early crewelwork, and the colors were various shades of blue, yellow, brown, and green. These rugs are rare.

In general, the three types of early American rugs may be

Linen tablecloth, brown and tan with portrait of Lincoln. About 1863.
NEW YORK HISTORICAL SOCIETY.

identified by their technique: patched with strips of cloth sewed on a homespun linen, tow, or woolen background; sewed with wool yarn through the background; and hooked with fabric or yarn through the background. The first patched rugs consisted of small square or circular patches of old woolen fabrics folded into fourths, or cut into strips and shirred, then sewed to the background. These rugs bear some resemblance to hooked rugs. The colors were those of natural-dyed yarns, and the designs were usually floral with wide scrolled leaf and flower borders. Some had baskets of flowers or houses in their centers, and others were made in geometric patterns.

Several types of rugs were made with yarn sewed through the background. Embroidered floor rugs, made in the early 1800's and similar to antique bed rugs, were made of homespun yarn sewed on a heavy background by a tent stitch or cross-stitch. The famous Pliny Moore rug in the Metropolitan Museum of Art was made by this method. Materials for the rug were grown, dyed, and spun on the farm, and the embroidery was done by daughters of the household trained in a Catholic convent in Montreal. Another famous embroidered rug was the Caswell carpet made in Vermont in 1835. It consisted of separate squares of different designs—flowers, birds, vases, cats, and human figures—sewed together. Because these rugs were expensive, only a few were made.

Rugs made by pulling the yarn through the background and leaving it in loops were a more common type. These were similar to hooked rugs; but the technique was different, and the underside revealed a line of yarn dashes, whereas the hooked rug yarn showed a continuous line with no open spaces. The colors of the yarn sewed rugs were those of natural dyestuffs: soft muted madder reds, yellows, greens, indigo blues, blacks, and browns. The designs were both geometric and floral. These rugs were made from about 1800 to 1850, and they are rare and expensive today.

The hooked rug, which is available and less expensive, is the most popular rug with collectors. Together with the ordinary braided rug, it is the typical country rug. Its foundation material was homespun linen, factory-woven cotton, or burlap sacking. Many rugs have been found the exact size of a burlap feed sack. The cloth for the hooking consisted of old garments cut into strips. Sometimes the strips were dyed to get the desired colors. Early home dyes were extracted from roots, barks, vegetables, flowers, berries, and fruits. Indigo and cochineal commercial dyes were not obtainable until the mid-nineteenth century. The design of the rug was sketched on the background, which was then stretched on a frame; the hooking was done with a hook resembling a crochet hook. Hooked rugs were made principally on the Eastern seaboard from Nova Scotia to Delaware, but some come from rural districts of the Middle West. The Shakers also made hooked rugs, including colorful knitted and hooked rugs with crocheted and braided borders. However, the typical Shaker rug was woven. Directions of Mother Lucy, a presiding minister of New Lebanon, say that two colors were sufficient for one carpet: "Make one stripe of red and green, another of drab and grey, another of butternut and grey. The binding yarn may also be of two colors." Most Shaker rugs found today are either rectangular or circular with stripes of the fore-mentioned colors.

The most interesting feature of the hooked rug was its design. There were rugs with geometric patterns, including

Handmade rug. About 1790. METRO-
POLITAN MUSEUM OF ART.

*Hooked rug, wool on canvas. Nine-
teenth century.* METROPOLITAN MU-
SEUM OF ART.

*Hooked rug. American eagle and
fourteen stars to commemorate admission of Vermont into the Union.
Nineteenth century.* METROPOLITAN
MUSEUM OF ART.

Early Pennsylvania wool rug. MET-
ROPOLITAN MUSEUM OF ART.

*New England rug with embroidered
flowers. About 1825.* METROPOLITAN MU-
SEUM OF ART.

block, log cabin, basket weave, wave and zigzag, and simple repeating circles, diamonds, and medallions. There were also floral designs of loose sprays or vases of flowers. Some of these had a center medallion and a scrolled leaf border. During the Victorian era the flowers became more realistic, and we can recognize the cabbage rose, the moss rose, and the lily. Animal designs used in early rugs also became more common at that time. These included cats, dogs, lions, stags, swans, parrots, birds perched on a nest, and a horse or pony.

Many hooked rugs showed regional and national influences. In Quebec the rugs were decorated with elaborate scrolls, floral wreaths and ribbons in the French tradition. The Pennsylvania Dutch preferred barnyard fowl, household animals, hex signs, and joined hearts. Rugs made in seaport towns had marine designs, including schooners and clippers riding the waves, and such nautical subjects as fish, waves, cables, and anchors. Women on the farm chose barnyard scenes of farmhouse and barn, while the villager might hook a rug with such buildings as the local church. Patriotic designs were another subject for hooking, and while these are not common, they are especially interesting. There were the American eagle, the American flag, the coat of arms of the United States, the Centennial design, and a rare rug commemorating the admission of Vermont into the Union. The welcome mat, including such inscriptions as "Welcome" and "Call Again," was also a favorite design, and rugs in this category bore such mottoes as "God Bless Our Home," "Home Sweet Home," and "God Is Love" and once in a while a verse. These were often semicircular, designed to be placed at a doorway.

Hooked rugs reached their height of popularity in the mid-nineteenth century, and long after the Civil War they were the principal floor coverings in rural districts. In fact, the vogue to hooked rugs endured until the end of the Victorian era. Later designs were often influenced by Currier and Ives prints and Brussels carpets. There were also patterns printed in *Godey's Ladies Book* and *Peterson's Magazine* during the 1860's. In the late rugs the colors were harsher and gaudier than those in the early varieties, and the workmanship was careless. The primitive folk quality of the designs gradually disappeared, and commercial designs replaced the quaint early patterns. By the middle of the nineteenth century the first commercial designs for hooked rugs were available. Metal stencils of tin, zinc, iron or copper were employed to print them in color on burlap by a peddler from Maine named Edward Sands Frost. Frost peddled his Victorian designs in New England and later opened a store in Boston and a factory. These Victorian designs are often found with a date. The Centennial pattern is dated 1776–1876. John E. Garrett located in Burlington, Vermont, and Canada. His broadside showed thirty patterns which are still followed in Nova Scotia.

Hooked rugs are found in all shapes and sizes from small rectangles to large carpets and stair runners. There were also square, round, and semicircular hooked rugs. The oldest had a foundation of linen, homespun wool, or unbleached cotton. Later rugs had burlap backgrounds. Rugs made of narrow strip cloth had a finer texture than those made on wider strips and since the loops were close together, they wore better. Pieces of old handwoven cloth signify the old age of a rug, and its colors are usually softer than later rugs. In buying old hooked rugs, the collector should consider the design, the color, and the fineness and evenness of the hooking. A stiff rug has probably had hard wear and may be rotten.

However, small holes or tears in a soft woven rug can be repaired, and genuine antique rugs are now so scarce that it is almost impossible to find one that does not show signs of wear.

The age of a hooked rug depends on the materials of which it was made. Old backgrounds of fustian, crocus cloth, and Osnabrig were used in late-eighteenth-century and early-nineteenth-century rugs. The best rugs came from Maine and other New England states and from Nova Scotia. Rugs made in Pennsylvania and the South, although interesting in design, were made of coarser materials and the workmanship was cruder. Pennsylvania hooked rugs were small, but because of their quaint folk designs, they are favorites with collectors.

Braided rugs were also made and used in rural districts throughout the nineteenth and into the twentieth century. They have stripes of contrasting color braided and sewed together, but no pictorial decoration. Braided rugs have become a popular item with manufacturers and are suitable for country living if the more expensive types of handmade rugs are not available. However, because handmade braided rugs are still being made in rural districts and because of the commercial output, they cannot be considered collector's items.

VII

Frontier and Western Antiques

After the Hunt *by William Harnett. Oil on canvas.* CALIFORNIA PALACE OF
THE LEGION OF HONOR.

THE LITERATURE of Western Americana has been a collector's field for many years, but the collector of antique objects has become interested in Western antiques only in the last decade. The scope of this phase of Western Americana is wide, covering the articles used by fur traders, frontier settlers, hunters, miners, lumberjacks, and last, but not least in collectors' interest, cowhands.

The fur trapper and fur trader followed close on the trails blazed by explorers, and for more than a century the territory back of the coastal settlements was occupied by the trappers, together with the Indians. The first American frontiers were set by the French and English trappers, and later the American fur-trading post became the first Western frontier settlement. Thus, the earliest group of Western antiques are the items associated with the fur trapper and the fur trader. In his dress, habits, and equipment, the trapper was influenced by the Indian. The costume of the fur trapper consisted of fringed deerskin jacket and pants, leather moccasins, and animal skin caps. The trapper sent skins back to the Eastern market, where they were soon in great demand. Leather clothing, such as breeches, were imported from England, but as early as 1743 Philip Freeman of London established himself in Boston and made and sold "superfine black leather Breeches and Jackets," according to the Boston *Gazette,* June 21, 1743. Leather stockings of different colors were also made and sold by Freeman. In the Boston *Gazette,* September 24, 1764, the following advertisement appeared: "A very great Number of the respectable Tradesmen of this Town have come to a Resolution to wear Nothing but Leather for their Working Habits, for the future, and that to be only of the Manufacture of this government." Buffalo robes and beaver hats were also in use although they became more popular later.

The early colonists also made extensive use of animal hides in making their clothes and household furnishings. Buffalo hides were used for robes, blankets, wraps, and moccasins. Lewis Farquharson, a dealer in buffalo skins in Albany, New York, advertised lots of 500 skins in the Albany *Gazette* in 1811. *Gazette* advertisement in 1801 read: "Cash paid for deer skins, 500 or less, either raw or russet dressed." Deerskins were used for hunting shirts, pantaloons, coats, leggings, and moccasins. Gloves were made from squirrel and beaverskins, and caps were created from raccoon, bear, fox, cat, rabbit, and woodchuck skins. Bearskins were also used for bedding.

Animal skins were in enormous demand by shopkeepers. In 1801 John Bryan, maker of muffs, tippets, and caps, advertised in the Albany *Gazette:* "Highest prices for bear, red and cross fox, mink, fisher and martin skins." The trade in buffalo skins lasted until the end of the nineteenth century. In a broadside of 1876, Hart, Taylor & Company, of Boston, which had been in business since 1860, advertised buffalo robes and coats, together with bear, wolverine, beaver, raccoon, genet and prairie wolf robes. Few of the articles of dress have survived, but there are small belongings of the trapper, such as buckskin leggings, gauntlets, leather bullet pouches, bullet molds, powder horns and knives, that are available for today's collector.

Knives: The skinning knife was necessary equipment of the trapper. The knives of the trappers and other frontiersmen were similar to those used by the Indians. They were heavy crude instruments, often resembling old kitchen knives. The trapper usually made his knives himself from old files or other pieces of iron or steel, or he had it then made by a local blacksmith. In general, they were large knives, with handles of wood or deer antler. The trapper's skinning knife had a curved blade, but other blade styles were also in use.

Many early frontier knives were imported; but by 1830 the Bowie knife had been invented, and this quickly became the American backwoodsman's favorite knife and remained so for many years. The original Bowie was made by Rezin Bowie for his brother James. A variation, designed a few years later by an Arkansas blacksmith, became the Bowie knife as we know it today—a large heavy knife with a single edge and a clipped point. The blade was about fifteen inches long. The gard was of iron or brass in the shape of an elongated letter *S*, and the grip was of wood, antler, or bone. The Bowie knife played an important part in the history of the West, and between 1830 and 1890 no frontiersman was without one. The knives were carried in a hand-tooled leather sheath and stuck in the belt. There were no marks or inscriptions on the early Bowie knives handmade on the frontier, and dating them is hard because there were few alterations

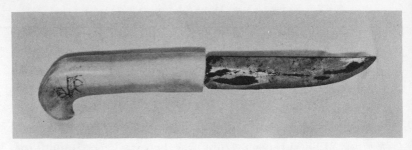

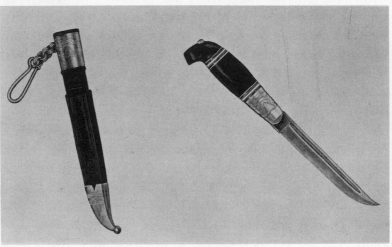

Trapper's skinning knife with bone handle decorated with etched elk.
SHELBURNE MUSEUM. *Trapper's hunting knife.* INDEX OF AMERICAN
DESIGN.

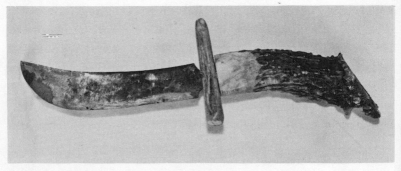

Trapper's skinning knife. SHELBURNE MUSEUM.

in their structure throughout the years. Many Bowie knives were later manufactured in England and exported to the American market.

In about 1840 another important type of frontier knife appeared. John Russell set up a knife factory on the Green River in Massachusetts and made a type of butcher knife that won immediate popularity as a frontier skinning knife. From this time on, the Green River trapper's knife was in greater demand than any other. At first the knives were stamped "J. Russell & Co./Green River Works" in two lines. Later a diamond-shaped symbol was added, and still later the mark was etched, instead of stamped. They were manufactured for many years, and the later knives are marked with both foreign and American makers' names. The blades of some had decorations and interesting inscriptions, such as the "Genuine Arkansas Toothpick"; a California knife made in the 1850's was marked: "I can get gold from quartz." Many knives also had decorative handles and hand-tooled sheaths. However, for the collector of country antiques the crude old blade with the handmade wooden, antler, or cowhorn handle is the knife of particular interest. The collector will be rewarded if he searches out West along the old Santa Fe or Butterfield Trail. The prices are not high, but the knives are becoming scarce.

Traps: The fur trapper depended for his livelihood on the excellence of his trap. At first he made his own wooden trap of poles or logs held by four heavy stakes driven into the ground. These were known as deadfall traps. Although these handmade wooden traps were popular, iron and steel traps were also used, and there was an ad for steel traps in the Knoxville *Gazette* as early as 1792. Daniel Boone used a steel trap, which he made himself. One of his traps is now in the West Virginia Historical Society. Boone also made and repaired traps in Missouri.

The old traps were usually handmade by the trapper or by the blacksmith, but they were also imported from Europe. Every trapper had a trap, which he may have made himself. Later, when the large fur companies were established, each trapper was provided with six traps. The fur companies usually employed their own trapmakers. For instance, the American Fur Company had a trapmaker named Miles Standish. Standish worked from 1822 until late in the nineteenth century. The first trap manufactured in the United States was made at the small factory of Sewell Newhouse in the Oneida Community, in New York State. Newhouse started with 3 workmen in 1855, but by 1872 his employees numbered 300. In 1865 Blake, Lamb & Company was manufacturing the Blake jump trap in Waterbury, Connecticut.

In 1875 *The Hunters and Trappers Complete Guide* published directions for hunting and trapping various animals, including buffalo. The book recommended the Newhouse steel traps. By then the Newhouse traps were being manufactured in eight different sizes and could be bought at hardware stores. The smallest was for the rat, muskrat, mink, and marten. There were also special mink traps, which could serve for trapping the fox and the fisher. The fox trap had two springs. An otter trap was also designed to catch beaver, badger, opossum, and wildcat, but there was a special beaver trap as well. The male bear trap could trap panther and Rocky Mountain bear, but for the grizzly bear and moose one had to have a "Great bear trap."

Early hider's scales from Wisconsin. INDEX OF
AMERICAN DESIGN.

Iron trap for large animal. SHELBURNE MUSEUM.

Traps were a necessity of the trapper's trade, but the frontier farmer and rancher also used them, both to protect himself from wolves, foxes, and other varmints and to catch game for food. Thus, many traps were made and used throughout the years. Moreover, because they are still being manufactured, the collector must beware of new ones. Old handmade traps bearing the maker's name are not plentiful, but early traps made by Newhouse and others should not be too difficult to locate. They are priced not only according to age but also according to size. Even the early household mouse- and rattraps and the literature concerning them are of interest to the trap collector.

Powder Horns: Powder horns were a necessity for the hunter. They were also used for miners and quarrymen to carry explosives, and they often served as canteens for water or for the vinegar used in sharpening scythes in the field. Ingenious pioneer housewives even stored their salt in them. But the principal use of the powder horn was for carrying gunpowder. Powder horns were of various sizes and types. They ranged in length from eleven inches to more than twenty inches. There were small priming horns and large family horns that hung in the cabin and were used for refilling the smaller horns. Powder horns were made from horns of cows, bullocks, and oxen. Most were homemade, but they were also sold by engravers called hornsmiths and by gunsmiths. Only selected horns were fit for engraving. Some were twenty inches or longer and beautiful in contour. Horns were engraved with a sharp professional engraving tool. Before the Revolution, when powder horns were imported from England, they were engraved with British coats of arms. American

*on bullet maker. Mr. and Mrs. William
ernon Ashley II. Bullet pouch of tooled
ather. Powder horn. 1865.* INDEX OF AMER-
ICAN DESIGN.

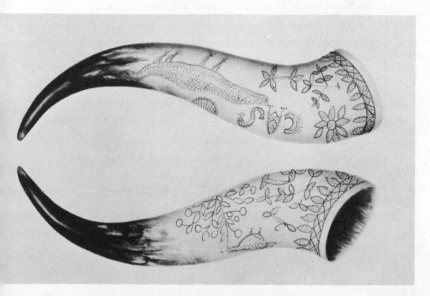

owder horn with engraved design. About 1870. INDEX OF AMERICAN DESIGN.

powder horns had historical scenes, and the collector's powder horns of the eighteenth century were engraved with maps, sketches of historic forts and towns, and battle scenes.

Maps included routes from New York to Canada via the Hudson and Lake Champlain, and the Hudson and Mohawk route to the West. There were also rare maps of New England and Pennsylvania. Some horns carried names, dates, and rhymes. Inscriptions were often of historical significance. The professional hornsmith dipped the horn in a yellow dye of butternut bark to bring out the grain in the translucent horn. Lines of the design were filled in with grease, wax, soot, or gunpowder dust to accentuate the engraving. Vermilion dye was also used for this purpose. Some horns were varnished or shellacked. The design on homemade horns was cut with a jackknife or pricked with a needle. These designs were crude and simple in subject matter. Typical were names and dates, animals, or primitive leaves and flowers.

In the nineteenth century powder horn designs included ships, eagles, flags, Masonic emblems, and figures of horses and deer. When not in use, the horn, together with the gun, hung above the cabin fireplace. When the brass powder flask was introduced in 1830, the powder horn was on its way out; but many hunters preferred the traditional horn, and as late as the 1880's plain powder horns could be bought in general stores. They were used with Kentucky rifles until the end of the century. Plain powder horns are inexpensive; but those with designs are higher in price, and those with historical scenes are beyond the purse of the average collector.

In the nineteenth century there was a revival in the use of animal horns. Besides serving as legs for late Victorian novelty furniture, they were mounted on hall racks and on mir-

Cowboy's outfit and equipment. About 1900. WITTE MEMORIAL MUSEUM.

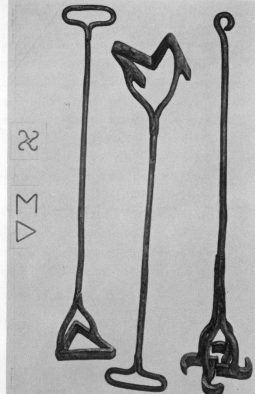

Early handwrought brands.
INDEX OF AMERICAN DESIGN.

rors and were even used as vases. Horn cups are also available for the collector.

Cowboy Gear and Equipment: In some part because of TV Westerns, items of cowboy gear have in recent years taken on a special interest for many collectors. Cowboy items for the antique collector include the articles of his dress and the harness and equipment of his horse and his job. These are for the most part nineteenth-century items, for the cowboy as such did not exist until the mid-nineteenth century when Spanish horses and Longhorn cattle from Mexico were introduced into the Southwest. Of course, the Spanish *vaquero* rode in California before the day of the cattle ranch. The cattle industry started in Wyoming and western Nebraska, along the Overland Trail to Oregon and California, at about the same time that it began in Texas.

The two great spectacles of the range cattle industry were the roundup and the drive, and the cowboy played the principal role in each. His uniform consisted of a cotton shirt and bandanna, a pair of overalls, leather chaps, a wide broncobuster's belt, a broad-brimmed Stetson hat, leather gauntlets, tall leather boots, and spurs. A rawhide quirt with a metal or wooden center hung from his wrist and was used as a whip, and a lariat of woven grass, horsehair, or rawhide hung from the saddle horn. A sharpshooter in a leather holster and a leather saddlebag for extras completed his gear. All this equipment is available to the collector.

Many of the older objects were made by the cowboy himself to fit his needs, and the decoration varied with his personal taste and ideas of decoration. There were old vests made of linsey-woolsey, and early cotton shirts were made of Texas

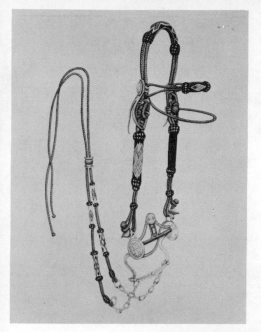

Hand-plaited bridle. INDEX OF AMERICAN DESIGN.

Bridle with silver insets.
INDEX OF AMERICAN DESIGN.

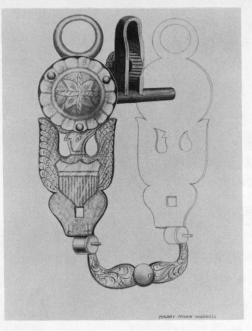

Bit with silver mountings, eagle design.
INDEX OF AMERICAN DESIGN.

Old iron bit. California. IN
OF AMERICAN DESIGN.

Hackamore bit used in breaking
horses. Ladies' leg design. INDEX OF
AMERICAN DESIGN.

cotton. The quirts and lariats were handmade. The 1880's were the heyday of the cowboy, but by the century's end, when the cattle industry passed into the ranch stage, both the dangers and the romance were over. In addition, although the costume remained the same, it was no longer handmade but was ordered from Eastern mail-order houses.

Among the many articles of leather for the collector of Western antiques are horse trappings. Saddles are perhaps too large for the collector of small items, but there were saddlebags, rawhide bottles, horse hobbles of twisted rawhide, leather stirrups, hackamores, bits, rawhide quirts, reins, and bridles. Bridles were made of braided buckskin or rawhide, and the metal chains attached to the reins were handwrought, as were the early iron bits. Some bridles and bits in the Southwest had silver buckles and buttons with the owner's initials, and designs on their medallions included buffalo heads. An extrafancy bit has a cutout silver eagle, and a Gay Nineties hackamore bit is tooled with nude women and mermaids. Some bridles were also woven of horsehair. There were also tooled leather racks with calf's feet and legs on which the harness was hung. These, too, were items of the mail-order catalogue of the 1890's.

The most interesting article in the cowboy's costume is the boot, and its attached spur. Before boots or chaps were used, leggings of tanned buck or soft skins, with flaring bottoms and cuffs at the top, were tied around the knees. These were often stamped with elaborate designs and in New Mexico they were embroidered with gold or silver thread or with colored silk. The leggings are also an interesting collector's item, but boots and spurs offer a wider field and are more readily available. Early boots were plain leather with

Spanish Colonial wrought-iron spur with huge spiked rowel. Eighteenth century. INDEX OF AMERICAN DESIGN.

Chihuahua spur inlaid with gold a silver. Nineteenth century. INDEX AMERICAN DESIGN.

Boot and spur with hand-tooled leather. WITTE MEMORIAL MUSEUM.

Spanish Colonial spur with etched line design. Eighteenth century. Worn by vaqueros *of Southwest.* INDEX OF AMERICAN DESIGN.

Spur with sawtooth rowel and cur shank, tooled leather. About 1 INDEX OF AMERICAN DESIGN.

only an initial or symbol in hand tooling or stitching on the cuff. Later the designs included leaves and flowers, stars, and geometric patterns. Some boots had mule-ear straps, and short boots were called peewees. Later boots were made with fancy designs and colored stitching.

Boots had high heels, and when the spur with its strap of hand-tooled leather was added, the cowboy's foot became a thing of glamour. There were many different varieties and sizes of spurs. Their shanks might be straight or curved. The size and design of the rowels and prongs varied. Spurs in different parts of the country varied in type, and not all cowboys in the same locality wore the same type of spur. It is their great variety that makes collecting spurs so interesting. Spurs ranged from simple spiked projections to those with fancy rowel spikes and gold and silver inlay which reveal a Spanish influence. Some years ago, when I was living in Mexico, I collected several dozen beautiful spurs which had geometric designs of gold and silver inlay. These were eighteenth-century spurs, and I bought them at junkshops and flea markets for a mere pittance. Spurs are still inexpensive. Of course, if you are lucky enough to find a spur with a tooled leather strap, that doubles the price.

Several types of common spurs are available today. The Chihuahua spur, which is similar to some of the spurs I collected in Mexico City, Morelia, and Guadalajara, was a heavy spur with a large rowel and was often decorated with gold and silver inlay. It is the type worn by *vaqueros* in the Southwest and in California. The most popular spur with the American cowboy was the OK spur, which dates to the early 1880's. It had a shank with a high arch and a small flower-like rowel. Cavalry spurs were of iron or brass with curved shanks, small rowels, and small leather straps. Some late spurs were made with eagles, horse's heads, or dolphins cast in the iron structure.

Cowboy boots required a bootjack, and many wooden homemade bootjacks are to be found in Western country shops. The later cast-iron and brass bootjacks, including the beetle, are especially popular with collectors. Other designs included a bulldog pistol, Naughty Nellie, and a lyre; some of these bootjacks were japanned and "Painted Fancy," and some were "Berlin Bronzed," as shown in a Simmons Hardware catalogue of 1881.

Branding Irons: Brand marks were the heraldic devices of the cow country burned on the cow's hide with a branding iron. Branding irons were of three types: running irons, which were simple hooked-end irons which could write on any brand; copper brand rings; and iron stamp brands, which had a long handle attached. The most common type, hence the most available, was the stamp iron. These brands were hand-forged by a blacksmith, and the brand and the handle were made in one piece, although some had wooden handles. Designs included simple letters, triangles, circles, hearts, anchors, numbers and such symbols as the Cross and Crescent, Bell, Sombrero, Fish, Pitchfork, Pothook, Hash Knife, and Lazy S and Lazy Double O. Mexican brands were more decorative and were a combination of geometric patterns, ornate scrolls, objects, and letters. The *La Junta Tribune Brand Book of Colorado and New Mexico,* published in 1886, included such brands as the Ladder, Wine Glass, Bible, Key, and Rocking Chair. Such famous brands as the Story Ranch brand, (the largest brand ever used in Texas), Bar X, Hash Knife, Diamond A, and Running W are rare and expensive because they are associated with the great cattle empires. Running irons and copper rings are also rare, but such simple brands as Lazy S, Turkey Track, or plain initials are comparatively easy to find and are inexpensive. Some of the most desirable from the standpoint of craftsmanship and decoration are those with graceful curves, such as Lazy S and Double O, Double S Wrench and Flying O, and Swastika. Such brands as Walking Box, Dog Iron, Pitchfork, and Hash Knife appeal to the collector because their names connote the lore of the cattle country. The handle end of the brand was also an interesting display of craftsmanship. Some ended in a flattened curved grip, whereas others were merely turned in a large or small hook. The collector should beware of the late welded brands and of the branding irons being used today.

Trunks: When the early settlers came to America, space on the small ships was so limited that little luggage was allowed. The chests of the colonists that have been preserved were made for storage and were related to furniture rather than luggage. Along with saddlebags, small wooden boxes with iron or leather fastenings served the colonists for luggage. Since journeys were made on horseback or by stagecoach with small accommodations for luggage, the trunks in use must have been small. The first American trunks were probably made to order by cabinetmakers or saddlers since they were not advertised until the end of the eighteenth century. One of the earliest advertisements was that of Halsted and Thompson, saddlers, who advertised "portmantuas, saddlebags, etc." in the New York *Gazette,* December 20, 1762. James Ettridge, saddler, advertised "portmantuas, leather bags, villeases for

Leather trunk with colored leather strips. San Fernando Mission, California. INDEX OF AMERICAN DESIGN.

Jenny Lind trunk with leather straps and medal bosses. About 1850. INDEX OF AMERICAN DESIGN.

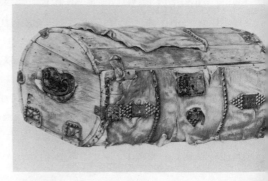

Trunk of pine boards covered with deerh Kentucky, 1812. INDEX OF AMERICAN DES

bedding"—the New York *Mercury* on August 29, 1763. After the Revolution there were many newspaper advertisements, placed by cabinetmakers, harness makers, and brushmakers, that included trunks. One of the first advertisements in New York newspapers to mention trunks was that in the New York *Independent Journal or the General Advertiser* February 2, 1785, placed by Joseph Adam Fleming, "who for many years carried on the Harpischord Making, Cabinet, Upholstery, and Trunk work in Europe . . . trunk work in all its branches, viz camp, coach, and portmantua trunks, ladies gilt ditto . . . canteens, valeeses, furr caps and band boxes. . . ." Gifford and Scotland, cabinetmakers, advertised "travelling desks" in 1791, and Cooper Trunk, Brush and Windsor Chair Manufacturer advertised in The *Diary; or Loudon Register,* April 24, 1792. Watson & Briskoe advertised a trunk and brush manufactory at 95 Maiden Lane, at the corner of Gold Street in The *Diary or Evening Register* on October 16, 1794. The advertisement of H. Miller, trunk and plate case maker from London, in the New York *Daily Advertiser,* December 2, 1796, read:

> Makes and sells all sorts of hair and brass mounted travelling trunks such as Post Chaise Trunks, flat and Spanish sumpters, hair and black leather portmanteaux, chaise, set trunks, and small trunks to go under the seats of stage coaches. Merchants supplied with all sorts of nests of trunks for the east and west India trade. Bottle cases, camp trunks, and travelling canteens; likewise light soal leather trunks to go behind a servant on horseback. Imperials made to fit on the top of coaches.

From the beginning of the nineteenth century American trunks were made almost exclusively by saddlers. In New

Leather trunk with brass nailheads. Early nine-teenth century. INDEX OF AMERICAN DESIGN.

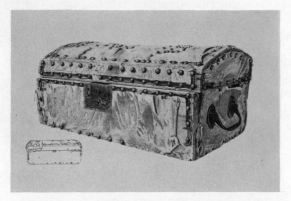

Pine boards covered with deerhide and trimmed with patent leather and brass upholsterer's tacks.
INDEX OF AMERICAN DESIGN.

Hand-sewed and tooled leather trunk. SHELB
MUSEUM.

York, saddlers Henry Stanton and John Smart advertised "Hard leather and hair travelling trunks" in ads from 1801 to 1804. However, in the large collection of trade cards of nineteenth-century saddlers in the Bella C. Landauer Collection at the New York Historical Society, none gave descriptions of the trunks which they made, and few showed illustrations. The card of William Bull, Wall Street, New York, depicted a small flat leather trunk, and later trade cards showed trunks of the Jenny Lind type. The first trunks were necessarily small. Those that were covered with horsehair, leather, canvas, or paper had a foundation of pine. Sometimes they were studded with brass upholsterer's nails placed in rows or circles or diamonds or with the owner's initials, a date, or a symbol, such as an eagle.

When the pioneers pushed West across the plains or took the long sea journey around the Horn, trunks became a necessity, and from this time on, there were many trunkmakers not only in the large cities but also in such smaller cities as Lowell and Springfield, Massachusetts; Cooperstown and Albany, New York; Charleston, South Carolina; and St. Louis, Missouri. The earliest leather-covered trunks were of deerskin stretched over pine boards and held with brass upholsterer's tacks and strips of patent leather braid. The following ad appeared in the Albany *Gazette* on April 5, 1813: "Trunk lost. Middle sized trunk covered in deerskin and without handles at end." Later sheepskin, pigskin, and oxhide were used to cover trunks. These trunks had cast-iron locks and handles and were lined with homespun cloth, old newspapers, or wallpaper, made by such wallpaper manufacturers as Pemberton of Albany, which advertised papers for trunks. Trunks covered with hides continued to be made through the middle of the nineteenth century. These hide trunks had both flat and rounded tops and are known as Arcon trunks. Those with handles on top were known as schooner or clipper trunks. These were used by the gold seekers who went around the Horn. The following ad with a cut appeared in the *Daily Alta California,* June 20, 1850: "Lost. A mahogany colored chest—came around Cape Horn."

The stagecoach trunk was made of leather with leather straps and handles and simple tooled lines. When Jenny Lind came to America in the 1850's, she had a leather trunk which curved in the center. It was bound with iron supports and had leather straps and handles at the ends. This became the popular American trunk in the mid-nineteenth century. The General Grant trunk, made of hickory covered with hide, and the Saratoga trunk came into vogue during the 1880's.

It is difficult to place the age of old trunks because the same types continued to be made for many years. The lining often gives the clue to dating. Old hand-spun materials or hand-blocked wallpapers suggest an early date, and newspapers often provide exact dates. The old hide-covered trunks may have spots of patchy hair, and the leather may be torn or discolored; but where other indications point to an earlier date, the trunk is worth acquiring as an example of pioneer craftsmanship. Although many of these trunks were made in the East, they were used for the trip West, and this fact together with their simple crude workmanship, places them in the class of Western Americana. True Western trunks, which were made in California and the Southwest, show a Spanish influence and were usually fashioned by mission craftsmen. They are of oxhide with braided geometric designs of strips of colored leather.

VIII

The Country Store

Grocery store showing pine counters, mailboxes, cast-iron coffee grinders, cast-iron and tin scales, painted tin spice, tea, and coffee containers, wooden and tin scoops, cast-iron twine holder, cheese cover, and wall telephone and shelf clock. INDEX OF AMERICAN DESIGN.

THE COUNTRY STORE is a romantic personal memory to
many people, whether it is the old store at Sandy Creek,
New York, whose fifteen volumes of account books are preserved at the New-York Historical Society, or Miner Grant's
store which is now in Old Sturbridge Village. It represents
a heritage and a tradition that has disappeared in most sections of the country. However, it's picture is familiar in the
many reconstructions and preservations in various museums
throughout the country. Moreover, a few antique dealers,
sensing the antiquers' interest, have set up shops as replicas
of the country store and grouped their items in nostalgic
array for the collector of country items. We are here con-
cerned with these items as they are available today. The old
general store has special appeal to the collector of small American country antiques of the nineteenth century because so
many of the articles that were once a part of the stock of the
country store are now available to the collector with a small
pocketbook. A short description of the store and its contents
will set the scene and suggest the supply of articles available.

The old-time country store was located at a crossroads or
in the center of a village. There was usually a porch or raised

Spice cabinet with stencil lettering. OLD STURBRIDGE VILLAGE.

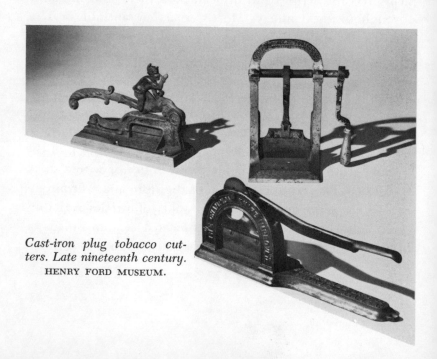

Cast-iron plug tobacco cutters. Late nineteenth century.
HENRY FORD MUSEUM.

platform in the front of the store. There in good weather a group of men would set on a wooden bench, telling tales or discussing politics. In cold weather they moved indoors to the captain's chair circling the potbellied stove in the center of the store.

The store's merchandise included groceries, hardware, household equipment, and toys, as well as clothing for men, women, and children. Indeed the goods included almost everything from buttons and bows to rattraps. The store also served as a general communications center. When not waiting on customers, the storekeeper was postmaster, and a small post office with a window and boxes for mail was set up in one corner of the store. One wall became a bulletin board with postings of community doings. The store's merchandise was displayed on the counter, on shelves, and in open barrels and boxes. On the counter was the large coffee grinder, a wire basket with fresh eggs, and a wheel of local cheese under a protective screen cage. The iron tobacco cutter stood ready to cut plug tobacco, and cigars were displayed in open boxes under a domed glass cabinet. Striped stick candy was in an open wooden pail. Other candy was displayed in glass jars. Square jars with heavy pressed glass tops or round jars with tin tops held horehound, rock candy, lemon drops, or licorice whips. Later candy beans were sold in souvenir glass revolvers, engines, ships, animals, and clown's heads. Open barrels held crackers, Fig Newtons and other cookies, sauerkraut, pickles, and oysters in season. Onions and potatoes in open sacks sat on the floor. The groceries were stored on shelves behind the counter, together with a decorated tin spice cabinet, such as one made by the Perfect Pantry Company, London, Ontario. Also available were china and crockery, including shaving mugs, spittoons, and toilet sets consisting of pitcher, bowl, soap dish, slop jar, and chamber pot. Although these sets were usually decorated in patterns, such as moss rose, some had romantic Italian scenery or English castles, and some were of decorated tin.

One wall of the store was lined with bins, drawers, and shelves. The shelves held patent medicines, Hood's Sarsaparilla, Plantation Bitters, and liquor. Tin lamps and lamp chimneys were stacked next to pottery pitchers, blue- and yellow-edged plates, bone- and stag-handled knives and forks, and iron and britannia spoons. Soap, shoe blacking, cartridges and shells, and Hess and Clark horse and cattle remedies were tucked away in a corner. Other shelves held piece goods—calico, cambric, linsey-woolsey, silk—trimmings, and dressmaker supplies, such as buttons, braids, fringes, ribbons, and whalebones. J. & P. Coats, Willimantic, or Clark's O.N.T. cotton thread was dispensed from the manufacturer's small walnut cabinet, which had two to five drawers stenciled in gold and colors. Peerless dyes were also dispensed in a walnut case, whose door was painted with scenes of an early passenger train and a camel caravan. The dealer's name and address "N. Spenser Thomas, Elmira, N.Y.," was painted in black letters.

The country store also sold children's toys, and at holiday time there was a large assortment, including dolls, wooden soldiers, tops, Noah's arks, pottery and iron banks, tin toys, wooden pull toys, and paper squeak animals and birds. Games included Lotto, Ten Pins, and the Geography Game. Books included readers, and spelling and arithmetic books. There were also boys jack knives, drums, harmonicas, and Jew's harps, and sometimes the stock included banjos and

Stromberg-Carlson early common
battery wall telephone in solid walnut. LEWIN'S ANTIQUE TELEPHONES.

Northern Electric of Cleveland heavy
rugged wall telephone. LEWIN'S AN-
TIQUE TELEPHONES.

Cathedral-topped crank telephones.
"Chicago Telephone & Supply Co.,
Elkhart, Indiana," and "Gold Elec-
trode" with shield-shaped transmit-
ter base and switch hook. LEWIN'S
ANTIQUE TELEPHONES.

Stromberg-Carlson wall telephone with
swivel horn-shaped transmitter, rare in
double box model. 1907 Western Electric.
LEWIN'S ANTIQUE TELEPHONES.

guitars. Many articles in the country store came in their own containers or fancy boxes, and these packages are also of interest to the present-day collector, so much so in fact that a later section will survey the field of old packaging. The storekeeper had small bags for loose articles and heavy wrapping paper kept on a roller upheld by iron supports, and a cast-iron beehive or openwork design holder for twine sat on the counter or hung from the ceiling by a cord.

Another regular feature of the country store was the wall telephone. Because it was sometimes the only telephone in the district, the phone was kept in constant use by customers. Messages were taken for the doctor, the preacher, or the undertaker. Today the old crank telephone that hung on the country store wall is a collector's item, and one dealer in Kansas is kept busy with his specialty—antique telephones. Since desk phones did not reach the country until the early twentieth century, these old wall telephones survived in country districts for many years and are still in use in some areas. Aside from their historical value, the solid walnut or oak cases and brass trimmed silver-plated receivers make attractive additions to a room furnished in country antiques.

All telephone cabinets had much the same appearance, although some had so-called cathedral, instead of straight, tops. Some had one long box with the mouthpiece set in the center and a shelf below; others had two boxes, and the mouthpiece was located on the board between. The cabinets were sturdily constructed with tongue and groove corners, and a good quality of yellow brass was used for the bells, cranks, switch hooks, and other metal parts. Early models of Stromberg-Carlson had brass-trimmed receivers, and their earliest receivers were of silver plate. The metal parts, however were covered with black enamel or nickel. The Kellogg case was the most decorative because it had more brass parts, a picture frame front, and a cathedral top. A few of these were made of walnut, but most cabinets were of oak.

The chief manufacturers of early crank telephones were the Western Electric Telephone Manufacturing Company, Kellogg Telephone Manufacturing Company, and Stromberg-Carlson Manufacturing Company. Other manufacturers were the American Electric Company, Premier Telephone Company, Swedish-American Company, B & R Telephone Manufacturing Company, North Electric Company, Cracraft-Leich Company, Chicago Telephone and Supply Company, and Monarch Telephone Company. Although there was a great similarity in telephone cabinets, most of the cabinets had a brass or bronze shield or plate engraved with the maker's name or some identifying trademark. Western Electric and Stromberg-Carlson models of 1882 are particularly desirable and rare collector's telephones. Although the crank telephone was a product of the 1880's and 1890's, Sears, Roebuck & Company and Montgomery Ward & Company still had them listed in their mail-order catalogues as late as 1917.

Wireware: One of the late-nineteenth-century products related to tinware and stocked by the country store was wireware. White lustral wireware was made in all manner of useful and decorative containers for almost every room of the house. Its largest manufacturer was Woods, Sherwood & Company, Lowell, Massachusetts, whose catalogue of 1878 listed hundreds of items. For the kitchen there were tea and coffee strainers, egg beaters, vegetable tongs, egg stands for cooking, sadiron stands, toast racks, oyster and pickle forks, dish drain-

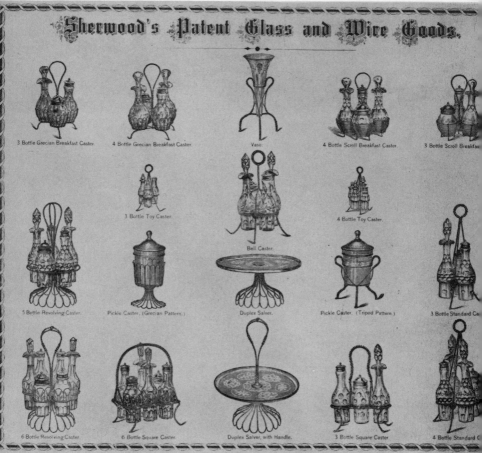

Sherwood's Patent Glass and Wire Goods.

3 Bottle Grecian Breakfast Caster.

4 Bottle Grecian Breakfast Caster.

Vase.

4 Bottle Scroll Breakfast Caster.

3 Bottle Scroll Breakfast

3 Bottle Toy Caster.

Bell Caster.

4 Bottle Toy Caster.

5 Bottle Revolving Caster.

Pickle Caster. (Grecian Pattern.)

Duplex Salver.

Pickle Caster. (Tripod Pattern.)

3 Bottle Standard Ca

6 Bottle Revolving Caster.

6 Bottle Square Caster.

Duplex Salver, with Handle.

3 Bottle Square Caster.

4 Bottle Standard C

WOODS, SHERWOOD & CO., Proprietors and Manufacturers, LOWELL, MASS.

Wire goods for the dining room table. About 1880. NEW YORK HISTORICAL SOCIETY.

ers, and dish stands, some with inserts of Minton tiles. For the dining table there were decorative fruit baskets, berry baskets, and cake baskets with glass liners and a tall epergne centerpiece holding a glass vase for flowers. Knife rests, napkin rings, match and toothpick stands, pickle casters, sugar bowls, and celery holders—all with flint glass containers completed the array for the dining table. In fact, all the articles which were made of plated ware for the Victorian dining table were reproduced in cheap wireware, which was especially suitable for country use. There were also portable dressing-table glasses, workbaskets, handkerchief and glove boxes, jewel baskets and watch stands, some trimmed with colored worsted. For the bathroom there were soap and toothbrush holders, and for the living room there were flower vases, music stands, newspaper racks and photo easels and stereoscopic view baskets. Hanging baskets for plants and moss completed the long list. All these articles, which were originally sold in the old country store, will be found today in junkshops and flea markets.

Coffee Mills: In the eighteenth and nineteenth centuries coffee making was a job requiring several different utensils. First, the coffee was roasted on the hearth. There were several types of tin roasters for use on the hearth. A rare cylinder type of roaster was set on an iron rod and held by a wooden handle, by which the roaster was turned. Other coffee-bean roasters were covered rectangular pans with long wooden handles. When stoves came into use, coffee-bean roasters were made for use on the stove top, and some had round bottoms made to fit into the stove hole. When the coffee beans were roasted, they were poured into a coffee grinder, or mill. Some early grinders were made of steel; others were of brass. They were set on

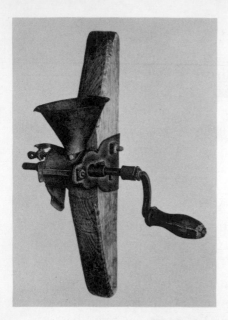

Wrought-iron coffee mill. Early nineteenth century. INDEX OF AMERICAN DESIGN.

National coffee grinder. Early twentieth century. INDEX OF AMERICAN DESIGN.

wooden boxes with a drawer below. A handle ground the coffee into the drawer. Then the grounds were poured into a pot of boiling water and boiled. When the coffee was ready, it was poured into a coffeepot for serving. The first coffee roasters and coffee mills were made by hand by the tinsmith. After some years, probably after the middle of the nineteenth century, coffee was no longer roasted at home, and the old coffee roasters were discontinued.

Home coffee mills with various improvements and patents were manufactured in quantity in the mid-nineteenth century although they did not appear in manufacturers or dealers catalogues until late in the century. Many of the early ones were made in France, but in an American hardware and cutlery catalogue of 1848, Wilson's, Mallory's, and Parker's coffee mills were advertised. Parker's wall mills, which had been patented in 1860, were advertised by Simmons Hardware, St. Louis, in its catalogue of 1881, as was Webb's Patent Standard Coffee Mill made by Landers, Frary & Clark, which had a fancy bronzed hopper cover. Parker's side mill and Wilson's improved wood-back mills were in the catalogue of Summers Hardware Company, Johnson City, Tennessee, in 1918, and several types of Parker coffee mills were available in catalogues as late as 1937.

The store-bought coffee mill was a combination of metal, iron, tin, and wood. The most common variety consisted of a square wooden box with drawer and an iron crank on top with a handle on the side. These were set on the table. Other models were entirely of iron, and some were small replicas of the large coffee grinder with a wheel handle which stood in the old country store. A unique coffee mill was called the Telephone. In the 1894 catalogue of C. M. Linington's, *Silent*

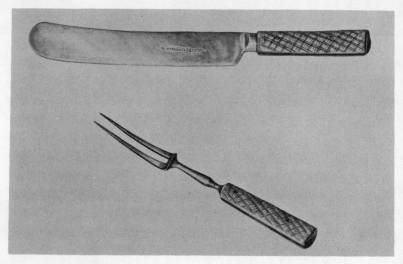

Bone-handled knife and fork with cut design. INDEX OF AMERICAN DESIGN.

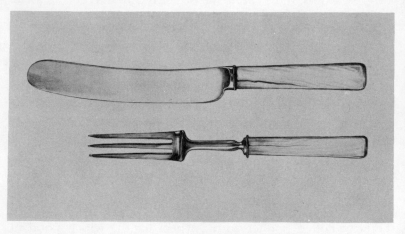

Bone-handled knife and fork. INDEX OF AMERICAN DESIGN.

Salesman, the New Telephone coffee mill was pictured. It resembled a wall telephone, was made of wood with nickel trim, and could be fastened to table, shelf, or wall. Later coffee mills were made of japanned steel, and several had glass canisters combined with metal. The coffee mill was made of hardwood, and the old ones had dovetailed corners.

Cutlery: Cutlery was sold at the general country store and at the hardware store as well. For many years plated knives and forks and britannia spoons made by James Dixon & Sons were imported from England. However, Britannia was made by American pewterers, including Ashbil Griswold, of Meriden, Connecticut, early in the nineteenth century. Britannia ware was a thriving industry in America until it was forced out by competition with plated ware in the 1840's. Although spoons and forks were made in America, the knife blades were usually imported from Germany or England. An 1848 catalogue of a Corning, New York, hardware and cutlery company included "ivory table knives and forks, American and English. Ebony, cocoa and self-tip, two and three prongs. Table steels, ivory, cocoa, and buck handles, nut picks, ivory and stag handles." Late in the century, when Rogers Brothers, Wallace Manufacturing Company, and Oneida were making plated knives and forks, several companies in America were manufacturing knives and forks with handles in imitation of French and German provincial wares. Knives and forks with ivory, ebony, cocobolo, rosewood, and metal handles made by Woods Cutlery were sold at Simmons Hardware in St. Louis in 1874. Landers, Frary & Clark, of New Britain, Connecticut, made knives and forks with iron, cocobolo, bone, rubber, and imitation stag handles. These were often decorated with brass, nickel, or pewter insets in the form of circles, crosses, and double crosses. John Russell Cutlery, Turners Falls, Massachusetts, also manufactured knives and forks with handles of pearl, ivory, Ivoride, rubber, steel, horn, bone, coco, and iron. The knife blades were usually of imported sheffield steel.

These were the types of cutlery used in the average country cottage and farmhouse and sold in the country store in the late nineteenth century. In 1900 Sears, Roebuck was advertising them in its catalogue. The popular knife and fork handles in the Pennsylvania Dutch country were of the staghorn variety; the forks had two long sharp tines. There were also handles of bone with brass and pewter insets of circles, hearts, and tulip shapes. This country cutlery may be found in shops in the rural districts of Pennsylvania.

American Packages: You can collect American packages dating from the middle of the eighteenth century to 1966. All have historical and social value, and many have artistic worth as well. Some were designed and labeled by the best-known artists and engravers of the day. Ink, soaps, creams, and perfumes of 100 years ago were put up in attractive packages that are of interest to the collector of advertising antiques today. Gunpowder, snuff, tobacco, coffee, tea, spices, and other household commodities were also packaged in boxes of various materials.

Some of the earliest containers were printed papers with labels pasted over the folded ends. Such a container held powdered ink dispensed by Joyce and Snowden of New York in 1790. The wrapper had an engraved design of an eagle with thirteen stars and an all-round border of laurel leaves. The inscription was in both French and English. This design

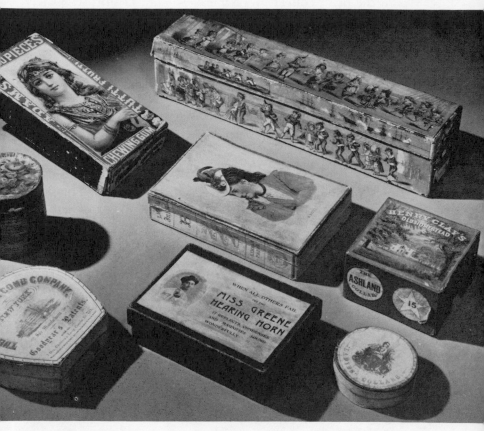

Cardboard containers with advertising. Bella C. Landauer Collection.
NEW YORK HISTORICAL SOCIETY.

was engraved by Rollinson and marked "Rollinson Sculpt." Needless to say, the wrapper is rare. One of the first imprints is in the print collection of the New York Historical Society. Another paper wrapper for ink powder had a design of an eagle on a globe and an Indian and a sailor holding an instrument. The paper was labeled "Superior Black Ink Powder Prepared by Willm. Kidder, Chemist, New York City, American Manufacture." Although no artist's signature was visible, the design and engraving were excellent. This rare label, which was made in about 1820, is now in the Bella C. Landauer Collection at the New-York Historical Society. Paper wrappers for N. & S. Smith, Prentiss Naples Compound, and Bear's Oil were made by Asher B. Durand in 1828. The bear's oil wrapper had an engraving of a bear. A paper package for "Thos. Haynes & Co., American Pin Manufactory, New York," has a design of an eagle and was engraved by the well-known artist, Alexander Anderson.

In the nineteenth century Anderson made many woodcut engravings for advertising packages. These were usually in the form of labels, which were put on glass bottles or tins or on paper wrappers for soap. They include the early label for N. Smith's Improved Blacking Cake, which had a design of an eagle. His design for the label of Patent Purified Windsor Soap pictured three feathers. A wreath of flowers surrounded the lettering for Pommade Fine, Dupuy. Other labels made by Anderson from about 1820 to 1830 included "Smith's Milk of Roses"; "Dr. Church's Vegetable Lotion"; "Huggin's Perfumery"; "Pear's Powder for Skin"; "Hamilton's Elixir for Coughs"; "Superfine Pomade Ointment"; "S. Holcomb's Chocolate"; "Caldwell & Fraser & Co."; "No. 2 Tobacco & Snuff"; "Peter Miller"; "Carbonic or Charcoal Dentifrice";

Tin containers for drugs. CAN MANUFACTURER'S INSTITUTE.

"P. A. Lorillard Chewing Tobacco," with a design of two Indians; "Best Virginia Snuff," with an Indian design; "Bear's Oil Pomatum, N.S. Prentiss, N.Y."; "Millefleur Soap," Jessame Soap, "Price & Cosnell, London"; N. Smith, "Prentiss Persian Otto of Rose Soap"; "Genuine Court Plaster, Cupid, N.Y."; and "Low's Oriental Saponacious Compound," with a picture of a lion. Anderson also did the striking label for "Swaim's Panacea," which showed a many-headed dragon being attacked by a man with a club. Indeed, the list of Anderson designs is so long and so comprehensive that it gives us not only a list of the products used in the early nineteenth century, but also the names of many of the New York shopkeepers and dispensers of medicine of early America.

Old playing cards and the packages that held them are also interesting to collectors. Anderson designed the package for Henry VIII playing cards made by Henry Hurd of London. During the Civil War unique Union Playing Cards were designed; they used a colonel for King, a goddess of liberty for Queen, a major for Jack, and eagles, shields, flags, and stars for the suits. These were made by the American Card Company, New York. Love scenes on playing cards from designs of French artists were also sold by L. A. Caswell of New York in 1864. Samuel Hart of Philadelphia made early playing cards, including the Eagle, Monitor, and Union sets.

Paper wrappers were also used over glass and wooden containers. Paper boxes were not used in wholesale quantity before 1839, and paper bags were not invented until 1852. However, wooden pill and herb boxes were made by the Shakers in the late eighteenth century. These had hand-stamped pine tops and bottoms with sides of shaved maple wood, bent and fastened with thread or wire clasps. They were often made in nests of oval or round boxes. There were long shallow boxes for garden seed, spice boxes labeled with dates or initials, and taper boxes. In 1820 the Shakers put up herbs as medicine. These handmade wooden herb boxes had printed labels with the name of the herb and a decoration of a lacy conventional border. Labels bore such names as "Summer Savory, United Society, South Groton, Mass.," Hardtack; Scull Cap Blue; Moccasin or Nerve Root; Dandelion Root; and Indian Hemp Root. One pill box read: "Dr. Phelps Compound Tomatoe Pills. Entirely Vegetable, Price $37\frac{1}{2}$ cents. None genuine without this label."

In 1806 Nathan Crary, Knox, New York, made shaved-wood boxes for spices, and many small pill and spice boxes were made of turned wood. Woven white ash bushel baskets were made for the sale of fruits and vegetables, and later buckets of woodenware, spruce or oak were used as containers for butter, lard, hard candy, and other groceries. Many of these bore the stenciled name of the grocer. There were also small boxes of turned wood that were used for various products. Shaving soap was put up in a wooden box in the nineteenth century, as it has been in the twentieth century. An especially interesting wooden box held cigars. In the inside cover was a humorous lithograph of men, a balloon, and a ship labeled *Pinafore*. There was also a turned-wood collar box made by A. Goodyear & Son with an engraving showing the seals of the original thirteen states.

Paperboard for hatboxes and the rims of Quaker hats was made as early as 1728, and until well into the nineteenth century, bandboxes and other small paper-covered boxes were made by hand. In 1830, however, Dyers Pocket Book and Fancy Paper Box Manufactory of Boston advertised in the

Boston Directory: "Large boxes for ladies dresses, cartons for gloves." Pasteboard boxes for dry goods were also made by N. Tarbell of Albany and several makers in New York City, including James Walsh, who advertised in 1832: "Pasteboard boxes of all kinds for Dry Goods, Druggists, Perfumers, Hair Dressers, Jewellers, Milliners and Artificial Florists." In 1839 Henry Barnes, a well-known bandbox maker of Philadelphia, advertised: "Bonnet, Cap, Curl, Comb, Shawl, Dress, Glove, Muff, Hosiery, Shoe and Fancy boxes. Wholesale & Retail."

It is generally understood that these boxes were made by hand. Whether or not they contained any printed advertising is not known, but they probably bore printed labels with the name of the goods and the name and address of the store. In 1831, the first paperboard mill was established in Chambersburg, Pennsylvania. Although Aaron Dennison is generally credited with the first commercial boxes, it was not until 1839 that he made boxes for use at his jewelry store and sold them for the use of other Boston jewelers. The demand was so great that he soon set up a small factory and was the first to use machinery in box making. In the beginning Dennison made boxes for pins, combs, keys, spectacles, pencils, needles, and paper collars and by 1848 had many well-known manufacturers as customers. By 1855 Dennison stand-up cardboard boxes were being used by many druggists, especially by George Plumbley of Philadelphia. J. I. Brown's troches were put up in boxes at around this date, and cosmetics, textiles, shoes, and stationery were also packaged in rectangular, oval, or round boxes with printed advertising on their covers. However, it was 1870 before stand-up boxes were used on a large scale, and then they were manufactured by commercial box companies in Chicago, Boston, New York,

Philadelphia, and Brockton, Massachusetts as well as in other cities.

Early folding boxes held tacks and such products as Union Horse and Cattle Powder, manufactured by C. E. Schubert & Company, of Pennsylvania, as well as ice cream, candy, and cookies. In the 1880's ice-cream boxes were decorated with lithographed scenes of flowers or birds and the printed name of the company and were carried by a string. Cookie boxes were rectangular or six-sided and were also held by a string. They were printed in one or two colors and had such gay designs as Santa Claus, red holly, mistletoe, and Little Red Riding Hood. In the catalogue of J. P. Brunt & Company, Chicago, old packages included cones and cornucopias with string handles and colored designs. These were made to hold raisins, prunes, apple, such cookies as animal crackers, or candy. Smith's Cough Drops were packaged in 1847, and Violet Cigarettes and Kirkman's Scouring Powder, with a picture of a Gibson girl, date from around 1890. Crackers and cereals were not packaged until later.

Most collars were packaged in cardboard boxes with labels printed directly on the box or a printed paper label pasted on. Beecher's Men's Collars had a picture of Beecher, Ashland Collars featured Henry Clay's old homestead, and Massachusetts Collars had a print of an Indian. Other collar boxes included the square Snow Flake Collar box and those for Gray's Molded Collars, Albany Paper Collar Co., Boardman Gray & Co., Hay's Patent Cloth Collar, Reversible Stitch Collar, Union Paper Collars, and Album Collars, which were packaged in a box designed in replica of an album. Ladies' collar boxes are rarer than men's, but there are some to be found. Spool cotton was also packaged in cardboard boxes, and these are especially interesting when found with the little spools of colored threads still inside. The various names on the boxes provide a history of the thread industry, and the same is true of the tiny pin boxes, which include glass-headed jet pins, mixed pins, mourning pins, and even hatpins. The colors and the lettering on these pin boxes is especially interesting. Eureka Toilet Pins, sold at (Marshall) Field, Palmer & Leiters in the 1860's, were arranged around a pincushion center. In 1880 the Eureka Pin package had a picture of an actress on its cover.

Early writing-paper boxes were often interesting in design. A rare box is the one with the colored picture of Adelina Patti marked "Laconia Initial Stationery." Not quite so rare is the one marked "Carlotta Patti, Aurora Initial." Oliver's Patent Glass Inkstand came in a cardboard box, and it is rare if found complete with glass inkstand. But perhaps the most intriguing boxes are the tiny old round and oval pillboxes with such markings as "Schencks Mandrake Liver Pills," "Rodney's Regulators," or just "Worm Lozenges." Early matchboxes with printed paper covers are also collector's items today, for matches now usually come in books or large boxes.

Many American containers were also made of pottery, and these are among the earliest labeled containers that the American collector can find. Jackson's Mustard was put up in earthenware jars in 1768 and advertised in Philadelphia papers. In the mid-nineteenth century, pottery jars for bear's grease and other cosmetics were made in England by Felix Pratt, and some were made later by Wedgwood. These potlids sometimes had attractive colored pictures of American buildings and scenery. Soaps, toilet creams, shaving creams, tooth powders, and other hairdressing and drugstore products were put up in heavy opaque glass or pottery jars. Wrisley's Saponaceous Shaving Compound was dispensed in a white china jar which had a black transfer of Independence Hall on its cover. Another rare jar contained Taylor's Saponaceous Compound and is decorated with a purple transfer print of a man looking into a mirror. Pure Ox Marrow prepared by Phalon, St. Nicholas Hotel, New York, had on its sides a colored transfer scene of cows. This jar is rare because Phalon was one of the famous early New York barbershops. The name of another early New York shop was on a square pottery jar with a white transfer, and the box containing Formodenta for the Teeth bears the name "Casswell, Mack & Co. New York and Newport." The jar containing Odonta Oak Bark Orris Toothpaste put up by Henry A. Choate, Druggist, under Revere House, Boston, had a lettering design in red transfer.

Many late-nineteenth-century cosmetics were packaged in blue and white Japanese pottery jars. One such jar was marked "Countie of Boston, Dainty Luxury for the Skin," and "Vantine's Oriental Nailstone" appeared on another. "Mrs. Conn Manicuring, N.Y." dispensed her products in a white milk glass jar. Edward Benneche & Brothers of New York sold ginger in a pottery jar marked "E.B." Caswell & Massy Taylor of Philadelphia put up their shaving soap in a china box with transfer of Washington crossing the Delaware on the cover. Samuel Horn's Lowell Soap was packaged in a white pottery jar with a blue-gray transfer of a Scotsman in kilts. All these boxes are not only interesting, but attractive as well, and although many collectors look for them, they are still to be had at a reasonable price, for they are more likely to be found in the secondhand store or junkshop than in the legitimate antique shop.

Appendix

Section I
TINWARE

FOR FURTHER READING

Gould, Mary Earle, *Antique Tin and Tole Ware—Its History and Romance*. Rutland, Vt., Tuttle, 1958.

McClinton, Katharine M., *Handbook of Popular Antiques*. New York, Random House, 1945; Bonanza Reprint, 1963.

—— *The Complete Book of Small Antiques Collecting*. New York, Coward-McCann, 1965.

Robacher, Earl F., *Touch of the Dutchland*. New York, A. S. Barnes, 1965.

Comstock, Helen, ed., *Concise Encyclopedia of American Antiques*. New York, Hawthorn Books, 1965.

Antiques Magazine. See Index for articles.

WHERE TO SEE COLLECTIONS

Old Sturbridge Village, Sturbridge, Mass.

Shelburne Museum, Shelburne, Vt.

Henry Ford Museum, Greenfield Village, Dearborn, Mich.

Henry Francis Du Pont Winterthur Museum, Winterthur, Del.

New-York Historical Society, New York, N.Y.

Section II
WOODENWARE

FOR FURTHER READING

Andrews, Edward Deeming, and Andrews, Faith, *Shaker Furniture,* New York, Dover, 1950.

The Horticulturist, 1846–1850, American Agriculturist, 1860–1880. *Journal of Rural Art and Rural Taste.*

Chronicle, Early American Industries. Williamsburg, Va., 1933–1966.

Earle, Alice Morse, *Home Life in Colonial Days.* New York, Macmillan, 1900.

Gould, Mary Earle, *Early American Wooden Ware.* Springfield, Mass., Pond, Ekberg, 1948.

Johnson, Laurence A., "Battle of the Baskets." *Chronicle,* Early American Industries (September and December, 1962).

McClinton, Katharine M., *Antique Collecting for Everyone.* New York, McGraw-Hill, 1951; Bonanza Reprint, 1965.

New England Farmer (1822–1846).

Nineteenth-Century Catalogues, Bella C. Landauer Collection, New York Historical Society.

Robacher, Earl F., *Touch of the Dutchland.* New York, A. S. Barnes, 1965.

Sloane, Eric, *Reverence for Wood.* New York, Wilfred Funk, 1965.

WHERE TO SEE COLLECTIONS

New York State Historical Association, Farmers' Museum, Cooperstown, N.Y.

Old Museum Village, Smith's Cove, Monroe, N.Y.

Old Sturbridge Village, Sturbridge, Mass.

Shaker Museum, Old Chatham, N.Y.

SECTION III

WROUGHT AND CAST IRON

FOR FURTHER READING

Chronicle, Early American Industries Association (1933 to present).

Lindsay, J. Seymour, *Iron and Brass Implements of the English and American Home.* London, Medici Society, 1927.

McClinton, Katharine M., *Antique Collecting for Everyone.* New York, McGraw-Hill, 1951; Bonanza Reprint, 1965.

Mercer, Henry C., *Ancient Carpenters' Tools.* Doylestown, Pa., Bucks County Historical Society, 1929 and 1951.

Sloane, Eric, *A Museum of Early American Tools.* New York, Wilfred Funk, 1964.

Sonn, Albert H., *Early American Wrought Iron.* New York, Scribner, 1928.

Wildung, Frank H., *Woodworking Tools.* Shelburne, Vt., Shelburne Museum, 1957.

WHERE TO SEE COLLECTIONS

Bucks County Historical Society, Doylestown, Pa.

New York State Historical Association, Farmers' Museum, Cooperstown, N.Y.

Pennsylvania Farm Museum of Landis Valley, Lancaster, Pa.

Smithsonian Institution, National Gallery of Art, Washington, D.C.

SECTION IV

COPPER AND BRASS

FOR FURTHER READING

Kauffman, Henry J., *Early American Copper, Tin and Brass.* New York, Medill, McBride, 1950.

McClinton, Katharine M., *Antique Collecting for Everyone,* New York, McGraw-Hill, 1951; Bonanza Reprint, 1965.

Henry Francis Du Pont Winterthur Museum, Winterthur, Del.
Old Sturbridge Village, Sturbridge, Mass.
Shelburne Museum, Shelburne, Vt.
Williamsburg, Va.
Riling, Ray—Powder Flask Book—New Hope, Pa., 1953.

SECTION V

COUNTRY POTTERY

FOR FURTHER READING

Barber, Edwin Atlee, *Lead Glazed Pottery*. Philadelphia, New York, 1907.

―――― *The Porcelain and Pottery of the United States*. New York, Putnam's, 1893.

―――― *Tulip Ware of Pennsylvania*. Philadelphia, Philadelphia Museum of Art, 1926.

Barret, Richard Carter, *Bennington Pottery and Porcelain*. New York, Crown, 1958.

―――― *How to Identify Bennington Pottery*. Brattleboro, Vt., Stephen Greene Press, 1964.

Calver, William L., "Historical Clay Pipes." *The New York Historical Society Bulletin* (October, 1931).

Knittle, Rheo M., "Ohio Pottery Jars and Jugs." *Antiques Magazine* (October, 1933).

Lichten, Frances, *Folk Art of Rural Pennsylvania*. New York, Scribner, 1946.

McClinton, Katharine M., *The Complete Book of Small Antiques Collecting*, New York, Coward-McCann, 1965.

Ramsay, John, *American Potters and Pottery*. Boston, Hale, Cushman & Flint, 1939.

Rice, A. H., and Stout, J. B., *The Pottery of the Shenandoah*. Strasburg Va., Shenandoah Pub. House, 1929.

Spargo, John, *Early American Pottery and China*. New York, Garden City Publishing Co., 1926.

Bennington Museum, Bennington, Vt.

Henry Ford Museum, Greenfield Village, Dearborn, Mich.

Metropolitan Museum of Art, New York, N.Y.

New-York Historical Society, New York, N.Y.

Old Salem, N.C.

Philadelphia Museum of Art, Philadelphia, Pa.

SECTION VI

HOMESPUN AND HANDWOVEN

FOR FURTHER READING

Davison, Marguerite Porter, *A Handweaver's Source Book*. Swarthmore, Pa., 1953.

Hall, Eliza Calvert, *A Book of Hand-Woven Coverlets*. Boston, Little, Brown, 1925.

Kent, William W., *The Hooked Rug*. New York, Dodd, Mead, 1931.

——— *Rare Hooked Rugs*. Springfield, Mass., Pond, Ekberg, 1941.

Reinert, Guy F., "Coverlets of the Pennsylvania Germans." Pennsylvania German Folklore Society, Vol. XIII, 1949.

Reis, Estelle H., *American Rugs*. Cleveland, World, 1950.

White, Margaret E., *Hand-Woven Coverlets in the Newark Museum*. Newark, New Jersey, 1947.

Henry Ford Museum, Greenfield Village, Dearborn, Mich.

Metropolitan Museum of Art, New York, N.Y.

Newark Museum, Newark, N.J.

Shelburne Museum, Shelburne, Vt.

Smithsonian Institution, National Gallery of Art, Washington, D.C.

SECTION VII
FRONTIER AND WESTERN

FOR FURTHER READING

Clark, Dan Elbert, *The West in American History*. New York, Thomas Y. Crowell, 1937.

Davidson, Marshall B., *Life in America*. Boston, Houghton Mifflin, 1951, 2 vols.

Mora, Jo, *Trail Dust and Saddle Leather*. New York, Scribner, 1946.

Leach, Douglas E., *The Northern Colonial Frontier*. New York, Holt, Rinehart and Winston, 1966.

Peterson, Harold, *American Knives*. New York, Scribner, 1958.

Schorger, Arlie William, *A Brief History of the Steel Trap and Its Use in North America*. Reprint from Wisconsin Academy of Sciences, Arts, and Letters, Madison, Wis.

Tryon, Rolla M., *Household Manufactures in the United States, 1640–1860*. Chicago, University of Chicago Press, 1917.

Tunis, Edwin, *Colonial Living*, Cleveland, World, 1957.

—— *Frontier Living*. Cleveland, World, 1961.

WHERE TO SEE COLLECTIONS

Henry Ford Museum, Greenfield Village, Dearborn, Mich.

New York State Historical Association, Farmers' Museum, Cooperstown, N.Y.

Panhandle Plains Historical Museum, Canyon, Tex.

Shelburne Museum, Shelburne, Vt.

Smithsonian Institution, National Gallery of Art, Washington, D.C.

State pioneer museums listed in Herbert and Marjorie Katz, *Museum, U.S.A.: A History and Guide*, New York, Doubleday, 1965.

Wells Fargo Bank Museum, San Francisco, Calif.

Witte Memorial Museum, San Antonio, Tex.

Section VIII
THE COUNTRY STORE

FOR FURTHER READING

Carson, Gerald, *The Old Country Store.* Toronto, Oxford, 1954.
Chronicle, Early American Industries Association, Williamsburg, Va., 1933–1966.
"Coffee Mills." *Spinning Wheel Magazine* (March, 1966).
Montgomery Ward & Company Catalogues.
Account Books of Grocery and Hardware Stores. New-York Historical Society.
Catalogues of Grocery and Hardware Companies. Bella C. Landauer Collection, New-York Historical Society.
Sears, Roebuck & Company Catalogues.
"Telephones." *Spinning Wheel Magazine* (April, 1966).

WHERE TO SEE COLLECTIONS

Henry Ford Museum, Greenfield Village, Dearborn, Mich.
Old Museum Village of Smith's Cove, Monroe, N.Y.
Old Sturbridge Village, Sturbridge, Mass.
Shelburne Museum, Shelburne, Vt.

Index